The little handbook of Windows Forensics

Andrea Fortuna – https://www.andreafortuna.org

Contents

Introduction

Some months ago I've got a **GIAC Certified Forensic Analyst (GCFA)** certification.

During exam preparation I've collected a lot of notes, and after the exam I've gradually organized them in an index based on topics emerged during the exam.

The result was not a simple braindump: for each exam question that remember, I've collect all notes taken during the preparation and organized them in an alphabetical index useful for a quick search during exam or day-by-day DFIR practice.

I've published the first version of this "handbook" as eBook on **Gumroad**, with unexpected results: a lot of users downloaded the PDF, and sends me priceless suggestions and typos reporting.

So, I've developed this final version with all integration and corrections.

Obviously, new suggestions are always welcome!

andrea@andreafortuna.org - https://www.andreafortuna.org

FAT Filesystem

Structure

Boot sector	More reserved sectors (optional)	FAT #1	FAT #2	Root directory (FAT12/16 only)	Data region (rest of disk)

Boot Record

When a computer is powered on, a POST (power-on self test) is performed, and control is then transferred to the Master boot record (MBR).

The MBR is present no matter what file system is in use, and contains information about how the storage device is logically partitioned. When using a FAT file system, the MBR hands off control of the computer to the Boot Record, which is the first sector on the partition. The Boot Record, which occupies a reserved area on the partition, contains executable code, in addition to information such as an OEM identifier, number of FATs, media descriptor (type of storage device), and information about the operating system to be booted. Once the Boot Record code executes, control is handed off to the operating system installed on that partition.

FATs

The primary task of the File Allocation Tables is to keep track of the allocation status of clusters, or logical groupings of sectors, on the disk drive. There are four different possible FAT entries: allocated (along with the address of the next cluster associated with the file), unallocated, end of file, and bad sector.

In order to provide redundancy in case of data corruption, two FATs, FAT1 and FAT2, are stored in the file system. FAT2 is a typically a duplicate of FAT1. However, FAT mirroring can be disabled on a FAT32 drive, thus enabling any of the FATs to become the Primary FAT. This possibly leaves FAT1 empty, which can be deceiving.

Root Directory

The Root Directory, sometimes referred to as the Root Folder, contains an entry for each file and directory stored in the file system. This information includes the file name, starting cluster number, and file size. This information is changed whenever a file is created or subsequently modified. Root directory has a fixed size of 512 entries on a hard disk and the size on a floppy disk depends. With FAT32 it can be stored anywhere within the partition, although in previous versions it is always located immediately following the FAT region.

Data Area

The Boot Record, FATs, and Root Directory are collectively referred to as the System Area.

The remaining space on the logical drive is called the Data Area, which is where files are actually stored. It should be noted that when a file is deleted by the operating system, the data stored in the Data Area remains intact until it is overwritten.

Clusters

In order for FAT to manage files with satisfactory efficiency, it groups sectors into larger blocks referred to as clusters. A cluster is the smallest unit of disk space that can be allocated to a file, which is why clusters are often called allocation units. Each cluster can be used by one and only one resident file. Only the "data area" is divided into clusters, the rest of the partition is simply sectors. Cluster size is determined by the size of the disk volume and every file must be allocated an even number of clusters. Cluster sizing has a significant impact on performance and disk utilization. Larger cluster sizes result in more wasted space because files are less likely to fill up an even number of clusters.

The size of one cluster is specified in the Boot Record and can range from a single sector (512 bytes) to 128 sectors (65536 bytes). The sectors in a cluster are continuous, therefore each cluster is a continuous block of space on the disk. Note that only one file can be allocated to a cluster.

Therefore, if a 1KB file is placed within a 32KB cluster there are 31KB of wasted space. The formula for determining clusters in a partition is (# of Sectors in Partition) - (# of Sectors per Fat * 2) - (# of Reserved Sectors)) / (# of Sectors per Cluster).

Wasted Sectors

Wasted Sectors (a.k.a. **partition slack**) are a result of the number of data sectors not being evenly distributed by the cluster size. It's made up of unused bytes left at the end of a file.

Also, if the partition as declared in the partition table is larger than what is claimed in the Boot Record the volume can be said to have wasted sectors. Small files on a hard drive are the reason for wasted space and the bigger the hard drive the more wasted space there is.

FAT Entry Values

FAT12
- 0x000 (Free Cluster)
- 0x001 (Reserved Cluster)
- 0x002 - 0xFEF (Used cluster; value points to next cluster)
- 0xFF0 - 0xFF6 (Reserved values)
- 0xFF7 (Bad cluster)
- 0xFF8 - 0xFFF (Last cluster in file)

FAT16
- 0x0000 (Free Cluster)
- 0x0001 (Reserved Cluster)
- 0x0002 - 0xFFEF (Used cluster; value points to next cluster)
- 0xFFF0 - 0xFFF6 (Reserved values)
- 0xFFF7 (Bad cluster)
- 0xFFF8 - 0xFFFF (Last cluster in file)

FAT32
- 0x?0000000 (Free Cluster)
- 0x?0000001 (Reserved Cluster)
- 0x?0000002 - 0x?FFFFFEF (Used cluster; value points to next cluster)
- 0x?FFFFFF0 - 0x?FFFFFF6 (Reserved values)
- 0x?FFFFFF7 (Bad cluster)
- 0x?FFFFFF8 - 0x?FFFFFFF (Last cluster in file)

Note: **FAT32** uses only 28 of 32 possible bits, the upper 4 bits should be left alone.

Typically, these bits are zero, and are represented above by a question mark (?).

Versions

There are three variants of FAT in existence: **FAT12**, **FAT16**, and **FAT32**.

FAT12

- FAT12 is the oldest type of FAT that uses a 12 bit file allocation table entry.
- FAT12 can hold a max of 4,084 clusters (which is 2^{12} clusters minus a few values that are reserved for values used in the FAT).
- It is used for floppy disks and hard drive partitions that are smaller than 16 MB.
- All 1.44 MB 3.5" floppy disks are formatted using FAT12.
- Cluster size that is used is between 0.5 KB to 4 KB.

FAT16

- It is called FAT16 because all entries are 16 bit.
- FAT16 can hold a max of 65,524 addressable units
- It is used for small and moderate sized hard disk volumes.

FAT32

FAT32 is the enhanced version of the FAT system implemented beginning with Windows 95 OSR2, Windows 98, and Windows Me. Features include:

- Drives of up to 2 terabytes are supported (Windows 2000 only supports up to 32 gigabytes)
- Since FAT32 uses smaller clusters (of 4 kilobytes each), it uses hard drive space more efficiently. This is a 10 to 15 percent improvement over FAT or FAT16.
- The limitations of FAT or FAT 16 on the number of root folder entries have been eliminated. In FAT32, the root folder is an ordinary cluster chain, and can be located anywhere on the drive.
- File allocation mirroring can be disabled in FAT32. This allows a different copy of the file allocation table then the default to be active.

Limitations with Windows 2000 & Windows XP

- Clusters cannot be 64KB or larger.

- Cannot decrease cluster size that will result in the the FAT being larger than 16 MB minus 64KB in size.
- Cannot contain fewer than 65,527 clusters.
- Maximum of 32KB per cluster.
- *Windows XP*: The Windows XP installation program will not allow a user to format a drive of more than 32GB using the FAT32 file system. Using the installation program, the only way to format a disk greater than 32GB in size is to use NTFS. A disk larger than 32GB in size *can* be formatted with FAT32 for use with Windows XP if the system is booted from a Windows 98 or Windows ME startup disk, and formatted using the tool that will be on the disk.

exFAT (sometimes incorrectly called FAT64)

exFAT (also known as Extended File Allocation Table or exFAT) is Microsoft's latest version of FAT and works with Windows Embedded CE 6.0, Windows XP/Server 2003 (with a KB patch, Vista/Server 2008 SP 1 & Later, and Windows 7. Features include:

- Largest file size is 2^{64} bytes (16 exabytes) vs. FAT32's maximum file size of 4GB.
- Has transaction support using Transaction-Safe Extended FAT File System (TexFAT). (Not released yet in Desktop/Server OS)
- Speeds up storage allocation processes by using free space bitmaps.
- Support UTC timestamps (Vista/Server 2008 SP1 does not support UTC, UTC support came out with SP2)
- Maximum Cluster size of 32MB (Fat32 is 32KB)
- Sector sizes from 512 bytes to 4096 bytes in size
- Maximum FAT supportable volume size of 128PB
- Maximum Subdirectory size of 256MB which can support up to over 2 million files in a singlr subdirectory
- Uses a Bitmap for cluster allocation
- Supports File Permissions (Not released yet in Desktop/Server OS)
- Has been selected as the exclusive file system of the SDXC memory card by the SD Association

Although Microsoft has published some information on **exFAT**, there are more technical specifications available from third parties.

Disk Unit Addressing

FAT saves file content in clusters. A cluster is a grouping of consecutive sectors (512-bytes each). When a file is described by the directory entries and File Allocation Table, the cluster numbers are used as addresses. The problem, is that cluster 0 is not at the beginning of the partition. Cluster 0 is in the Data Area, which is after the super block and File Allocation Tables and can be hundreds of sectors into the partition. This creates a problem because if The Sleuth Kit were to use clusters as the addressable units, then there would be no way to identify the non-"data area" sectors.

This problem was solved by making the sector as the addressable unit, instead of the cluster. When a file is described (using istat for example), the sector addresses are given. In the output of fsstat, the File Allocation Table contents are displayed in sectors and when using *blkls -l*, the sector status is given.

This actually makes manual data recovery easier because one can use 'dd' to carve out data using the sector addresses. If clusters were given, the user would have to translate the Data Area address to sectors before carving out data.

Metadata Addressing

FAT describes its files in a directory entry structure, which is contained in the sectors allocated by the parent directory. The directory entry structures have a fixed size of 32-bytes, not addressed, and can exist anywhere in the partition. The Sleuth Kit needs some form of Metadata Address for each file, so this became a problem. Also, the root directory does not have a directory entry. In other words, there is no descriptive information for the root directory.

The solution to this problem was to use the same method that is used in many UNIX implementations. Each sector in the data area is treated as though it could be full of directory entries. As each sector is 512-bytes and each directory entry is 32-bytes, each sector could contain 16 entries. To keep things similar to UNIX, the root directory is given the value of 2. The first 32-bytes of the first sector in the data area are addressed as 3, the second 32-bytes of the sector are 4 etc. The Sleuth Kit will scan through the sectors and identify which ones actually contain directory entries.

This method will produce large gaps of addresses between used address values.

Notes on Timezones

FAT does not store the file times in the delta format that UNIX does. Instead of saving the difference in time from GMT, FAT simply saves the raw hour, minute, and second values. The Sleuth Kit stores all times in the UNIX GMT offset format and will translate the FAT time to the UNIX offset. This uses the current timezone value when identify the GMT offset.

If the tool displays the time in a nice ASCII format, the same timezone will be used to translate the offset value into a date. Therefore, you can use any timezone value and the time will not change (just the timezone name). On the other hand, if you use a tool such as ils or fls -m, which display the time in the offset format, then it will have the offset of the current timezone or the one specified with '-z'. Therefore, ensure that the same '-z' argument is used with mactime to display the correct time in the timeline.

General Notes on Time

Each file in FAT can store up to three times (last accessed, written, and created). The last written time is the only 'required' time and is accurate to a second. The create time is optional and is accurate to the tenth of a second (Note that I have seen several system directories in Windows that have a create time of 0). The last access time is also optional and is only accurate to the day (so the times are 00:00:00 in The Sleuth Kit).

Sentinel Timestamps

Date	Interpretation
January 1, 0001	The value 0 as a CLR System.DateTime.
January 1, 1601	The value 0 as a Win32 FILETIME.
December 29/30, 1899	The value -1 or 0 as an OLE automation date.
December 13, 1901	The value 0x80000000 as a time_t.
December 31, 1969 January 1, 1970	The value -1 or 0 as a time_t.

January 1, 1980	The beginning of the DOS date/time era. (Unlikely to be encountered since 0 is not a valid DOS date/time value.)
January 19, 2038	The value 0x7FFFFFFF as a time_t.
February 7, 2106	The value 0xFFFFFFFF as a time_t.
September 14, 30828	The value 0x7FFFFFFF`FFFFFFFF as a FILETIME.

All of these special values have one thing in common: If you see them, it's probably a bug.

Typically, they will arise when somebody fails to do proper error checking and ends up treating an error code as if it were a valid return value. (The special values 0, -1, and 0xFFFFFFFF are often used as error codes.)

*The FAT filesystem **does not store an access time (just the date)**. It stores timestamp values in local time, and does not update a file's modification timestamp when the file is copied.*

References

- https://wiki.sleuthkit.org/index.php?title=FAT_Implementation_Notes
- https://blogs.msdn.microsoft.com/oldnewthing/20051028-29/?p=33573/
- http://www.forensicswiki.org/wiki/FAT
- https://www.sans.org/reading-room/whitepapers/forensics/reverse-engineering-microsoft-exfat-file-system-33274

NTFS Filesystem

The **New** **T**echnology **F**ile **S**ystem (**NTFS**) is a file system developed and introduced by Microsoft in 1995 with Windows NT as a replacement for the FAT file system.

Versions

Microsoft has released five versions of NTFS:

- **v1.0**: Released with Windows NT 3.1 in 1993.
  v1.0 is incompatible with v1.1 and newer: Volumes written by Windows NT 3.5x cannot be read by Windows NT 3.1 until an update (available on the NT 3.5x installation media) is installed.
- **v1.1**: Released with Windows NT 3.51 in 1995.
  Supports compressed files, named streams and access control lists
- **v1.2**: Released with Windows NT 4.0 in 1996.
  Supports security descriptors. Commonly called NTFS 4.0 after the OS release.
- **v3.0**: Released with Windows 2000.
  Supports disk quotas, Encrypting File System, sparse files, reparse points, update sequence number (USN) journaling, the $Extend folder and its files.
  Reorganized security descriptors so that multiple files using the same security setting can share the same descriptor.
  Commonly called NTFS 5.0 after the OS release.
- **v3.1**: Released with Windows XP in October 2001.
  Expanded the Master File Table (MFT) entries with redundant MFT record number (useful for recovering damaged MFT files).
  Commonly called NTFS 5.1 after the OS release

Structure

NTFS is optimized for 4 KB clusters, but supports a maximum cluster size of 64 KB.

Volume Size	NTFS Cluster Size
7 megabytes (MB)–512 MB	512 bytes
513 MB–1,024 MB	1 KB
1,025 MB–2 GB	2 KB
2 GB–2 terabytes	4 KB

The maximum **NTFS** volume size that the specification can support is 2^{64} – 1clusters, but not all implementations achieve this theoretical maximum, as discussed below.

The maximum **NTFS** volume size implemented in **Windows XP Professional** is 2^{32} – 1 clusters, partly due to partition table limitations.

Using the default cluster size of 4 KB, the maximum **NTFS** volume size is 16 TB minus 4 KB.

Both of these are vastly higher than the **128 GB** limit in **Windows XP SP1**.

Because partition tables on master boot record (**MBR**) disks support only partition sizes up to 2 TB, multiple GUID Partition Table (GPT or "dynamic") volumes must be combined to create a single NTFS volume larger than 2 TB.

Booting from a GPT volume to a **Windows** environment in a **Microsoft** supported way requires a system with Unified Extensible Firmware Interface (UEFI) and **64-bit support**.

Description	Limit
Maximum file size	Architecturally: 16 exabytes minus 1 KB (2^{64} bytes minus 1 KB) Implementation: 16 terabytes minus 64 KB (2^{44} bytes minus 64 KB)

Maximum volume size	Architecturally: 2^{64} clusters minus 1 cluster Implementation: 256 terabytes minus 64 KB (2^{32} clusters minus 1 cluster)
Files per volume	4,294,967,295 (2^{32} minus 1 file)

The **NTFS** maximum theoretical limit on the size of individual files is 16 EiB (16 × 1024^6 or 2^{64} bytes) minus 1 KB, which totals to **18,446,744,073,709,550,592 bytes**.

With **Windows 8** and **Windows Server 2012**, the maximum *implemented* file size is 256 TB minus 64 KB or **281,474,976,645,120 bytes.**

Master File Table

In NTFS, all file, directory and metafile data—file name, creation date, access permissions (by the use of access control lists), and size—are stored as metadata in the **Master File Table** (**MFT**).

This abstract approach allowed easy addition of file system features during **Windows NT**'s development and also enables fast file search software such as Everything to locate named local files and folders included in the **MFT** very quickly, without requiring any other index.

The **MFT** structure supports algorithms which minimize disk fragmentation. A directory entry consists of a filename and a "file ID", which is the record number representing the file in the Master File Table. The file ID also contains a reuse count to detect stale references.

Two copies of the **MFT** are stored in case of corruption. If the first record is corrupted, **NTFS** reads the second record to find the **MFT** mirror file. Locations for both files are stored in the boot sector.

Metafiles

NTFS contains several files that define and organize the file system. In all respects, most of these files are structured like any other user file ($Volume being the most peculiar), but are not of direct interest to file system clients. These metafiles define files, back up critical file system data, buffer file system changes, manage free space allocation, satisfy BIOS expectations, track bad allocation units, and store security and disk space usage information. All content is in an unnamed data stream, unless otherwise indicated.

Segment Number	File Name	Purpose
0	$MFT	Describes all files on the volume, including file names, timestamps, stream names, and lists of cluster numbers where data streams reside, indexes, security identifiers, and file attributes like "read only", "compressed", "encrypted", etc.

1	$MFTMirr	Duplicate of the first vital entries of $MFT, usually 4 entries (4 Kilobytes).
2	$LogFile	Contains transaction log of file system metadata changes.
3	$Volume	Contains information about the volume, namely the volume object identifier, volume label, file system version, and volume flags (mounted, chkdsk requested, requested $LogFile resize, mounted on NT 4, volume serial number updating, structure upgrade request). This data is not stored in a data stream, but in special MFT attributes: If present, a volume object ID is stored in an $OBJECT_ID record; the volume label is stored in a $VOLUME_NAME record, and the remaining volume data is in a $VOLUME_INFORMATION record. Note: volume serial number is stored in file $Boot (below).
4	$AttrDef	A table of MFT attributes that associates numeric identifiers with names.
5	.	Root directory. Directory data is stored in $INDEX_ROOT and $INDEX_ALLOCATION attributes both named $I30.
6	$Bitmap	An array of bit entries: each bit indicates whether its corresponding cluster is used (allocated) or free (available for allocation).
7	$Boot	Volume boot record. This file is always located at the first clusters on the volume. It contains bootstrap code and a BIOS parameter block including a volume serial number and cluster numbers of $MFT and $MFTMirr.
8	$BadClus	A file that contains all the clusters marked as having bad sectors. This file simplifies cluster management by the chkdsk utility, both as a place to put newly discovered bad sectors, and for identifying unreferenced clusters. This file contains two data streams, even on volumes with no bad sectors: an unnamed stream contains bad sectors—it is

		zero length for perfect volumes; the second stream is named $Bad and contains all clusters on the volume not in the first stream.
9	$Secure	Access control list database that reduces overhead having many identical ACLs stored with each file, by uniquely storing these ACLs only in this database (contains two indices: $SII *(Standard_Information ID)* and $SDH *(Security Descriptor Hash)*, which index the stream named $SDS containing actual ACL table).
10	$UpCase	A table of unicode uppercase characters for ensuring case-insensitivity in Win32 and DOS namespaces.
11	$Extend	A file system directory containing various optional extensions, such as $Quota, $ObjId, $Reparse or $UsnJrnl.
12–23	Reserved for $MFT extension entries. Extension entries are additional MFT records that contain additional attributes that do not fit in the primary record. This could occur if the file is sufficiently fragmented, has many streams, long filenames, complex security, or other rare situations.	
24	$Extend\$Quota	Holds disk quota information. Contains two index roots, named $O and $Q.
25	$Extend\$ObjId	Holds link tracking information. Contains an index root and allocation named $O.
26	$Extend\$Reparse	Holds reparse point data (such as symbolic links). Contains an index root and allocation named $R.
27—	Beginning of regular file entries.	

These metafiles are treated specially by Windows, handled directly by the NTFS.SYS driver and are difficult to directly view: special purpose-built tools are needed.

Attributes

For each file (or directory) described in the MFT record, there is a linear repository of stream descriptors (also named *attributes*), packed together in one or more MFT records (containing the so-called *attributes list*), with extra padding to fill the fixed 1 KB size of every MFT record, and that fully describes the effective streams associated with that file.

Each attribute has an attribute type (a fixed-size integer mapping to an attribute definition in file $AttrDef), an optional attribute name (for example, used as the name for an alternate data stream), and a value, represented in a sequence of bytes.

For NTFS, the standard data of files, the alternate data streams, or the index data for directories are stored as attributes.

Resident and non-resident attributes

According to **$AttrDef**, some attributes can be either resident or non-resident. The $DATA attribute, which contains file data, is such an example. When the attribute is resident (which is represented by a flag), its value is stored directly in the MFT record. Otherwise, clusters are allocated for the data, and the cluster location information is stored as data runs in the attribute.

Some resident attributes:

- **$STANDARD_INFORMATION**: Contains MAC times, security ID, Owners ID, permissions in DOS format, and quota data.
- **$FILE_NAME**: Contains the file name in UNICODE, as well as additional MAC times, and the MFT entry of the parent directory.
- **$OBJECT_ID**: Identifiers regarding the files original Object ID, its birth Volume ID, and Domain ID.

Anonymous attributes

Some attribute types cannot have a name and must remain anonymous.

This is the case for the standard attributes, or for the preferred NTFS "filename" attribute type, or the "short filename" attribute type, when it is also present (for compatibility with DOS-like applications, see below). It is also possible for a file to contain only a short filename, in which case it will be the preferred one, as listed in the Windows Explorer.

The filename attributes stored in the attribute list do not make the file immediately accessible through the hierarchical file system. In fact, all the filenames must be indexed separately in at least one separate directory on the same volume, with its own MFT record and its own security descriptors and attributes, that will reference the MFT record number for that file. This allows the same file or directory to be "hardlinked" several times from several containers on the same volume, possibly with distinct filenames.

The default data stream of a regular file is a stream of type $DATA but with an anonymous name, and the ADSs are similar but must be named.

On the opposite, the default data stream of directories has a distinct type, but are not anonymous: they have an attribute name ("$I30" in NTFS 3+) that reflects its indexing format.

Last Access Time

Each file and folder on an NTFS volume contains an attribute called Last Access Time.

This attribute shows when the file or folder was last accessed, such as when a user performs a folder listing, adds files to a folder, reads a file, or makes changes to a file. The most up-to-date Last Access Time is always stored in memory and is eventually written to disk within two places:

- The file's attribute, which is part of its MFT record.
- A directory entry for the file. The directory entry is stored in the folder that contains the file. Files with multiple hard links have multiple directory entries.

The Last Access Time on disk is not always current because NTFS looks for a one-hour interval before forcing the Last Access Time updates to disk.

Windows NT and its descendants keep internal timestamps as UTC and make the appropriate conversions for display purposes; all NTFS timestamps are in UTC.

For historical reasons, the versions of Windows that do not support NTFS all keep time internally as local zone time, and therefore so do all file systems – other than NTFS – that are supported by current versions of Windows. This means that when files are copied or moved between NTFS and non-NTFS partitions, the OS needs to convert timestamps on the fly.

NTFS also delays writing the Last Access Time to disk when users or programs perform read-only operations on a file or folder, such as listing the folder's contents or reading (but not changing) a file in the folder.

If the Last Access Time is kept current on disk for read operations, all read operations become write operations, which impacts NTFS performance.

Within the file's attribute

NTFS typically updates a file's attribute on disk if the current Last Access Time in memory differs by more than an hour from the Last Access Time stored on disk, or when all in-memory references to that file are gone, whichever is more recent. For example, if a file's current Last Access Time is 1:00 P.M., and you read the file at 1:30 P.M., NTFS does not update the Last Access Time. If you read the file again at 2:00 P.M., NTFS updates the Last Access Time in the file's attribute to reflect 2:00 P.M. because the file's attribute shows 1:00 P.M. and the in-memory Last Access Time shows 2:00 P.M.

Within a directory entry for a file

NTFS updates the directory entry for a file during the following events:

- When NTFS updates the file's Last Access Time and detects that the Last Access Time for the file differs by more than an hour from the Last Access Time stored in the file's directory entry. This update typically occurs after a program closes the handle used to access a file within the directory. If the program holds the handle open for an extended time, a lag occurs before the change appears in the directory entry.
- When NTFS updates other file attributes such as Last Modify Time, and a Last Access Time update is pending. In this case, NTFS updates the Last Access Time along with the other updates without additional performance impact.

If you have an NTFS volume with a high number of folders or files, and a program is running that briefly accesses each of these in turn, the I/O bandwidth used to generate the Last Access Time updates can be a significant percentage of the overall I/O bandwidth.

Alternate Data streams

ADS were introduced starting in Windows NT 3.1. in order to add "extra" information to the files without altering the original file format or content.

This extra information is the metadata about the file. This metadata is arranged in the form of streams that attach to the main data stream (the stream which is visible to a normal user).

For example, one file stream could hold the security information for the file such as access permissions while another one could hold data that describes the purpose of the file, its author and the MAC times.

Alternate streams are not listed in Windows Explorer, and their size is not included in the file's size. When the file is copied or moved to another file system without ADS support the user is warned that alternate data streams cannot be preserved. No such warning is typically provided if the file is attached to an e-mail, or uploaded to a website.

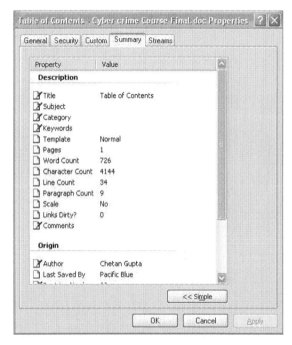

Many applications use ADS to store attributes of a file in them: for example, if you create a word document and right click and go into its properties, you can see a summary page which contains information that contains metadata about the data contained in the file. The metadata includes the author of the document, word count, no of pages and so on.

This summary information is attached to the file via ADS.

All files on an NTFS volume consist of at least one stream - the main stream – this is the normal, viewable file in which data is stored.

The full name of a stream is of the form below.

```
<filename>:<stream name>:<stream type>
```

The default data stream has no name.

That is, the fully qualified name for the default stream for a file called "sample.txt" is "**sample.txt::$DATA**" since "**sample.txt**" is the name of the file and "**$DATA**" is the stream type.

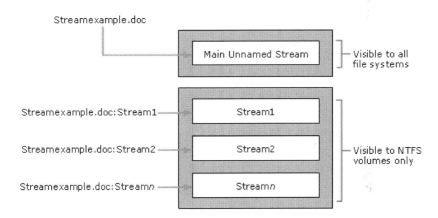

A user can create a named stream in a file and "$DATA" as a legal name.

That means that for this stream, the full name is **sample.txt:$DATA:$DATA**. If the user had created a named stream of name "bar", its full name would be sample.txt:bar:$DATA.

Any legal characters for a file name are legal for the stream name (including spaces).

In the case of directories, there is no default data stream, but there is a default directory stream.

Directories are the stream type $INDEX_ALLOCATION. The default stream name for the type $INDEX_ALLOCATION (a directory stream) is *$I30*.

The following are equivalent:

```
Dir C:\Users
Dir C:\Users:$I30:$INDEX_ALLOCATION
Dir C:\Users::$INDEX_ALLOCATION
```

Although directories do not have a default data stream, they can have named data streams.

These alternate data streams are not normally visible, but can be observed from a command line using the /R option of the DIR command.

Known Alternate Stream Names

- **Zone.Identifier**: **Windows Internet Explorer** uses this stream for storage of URL security zones.
  (*1=Intranet, 2=Trusted, 3=Internet, 4=Untrusted*)
- **OECustomProperty**: Used by **Outlook Express** for storage of custom properties related to email files.
- **encryptable**: Windows Shell uses the stream to store attributes relating to thumbnails in the thumbnails database.
- **favicon**: Used by **Windows Internet Explorer** for storing favorite ICONs for web pages.
- **AFP_AfpInfo** and **AFP_Resource**: Used for compatibility with **Macintosh** operating system property lists.
- **{59828bbb-3f72-4c1b-a420-b51ad66eb5d3}.XPRESS**: Used during remote differential compression.

Sparse Files

A sparse file has an attribute that causes the I/O subsystem to allocate only meaningful (nonzero) data. Nonzero data is allocated on disk, and non-meaningful data (large strings of data composed of zeros) is not. When a sparse file is read, allocated data is returned as it was stored; non-allocated data is returned, by default, as zeros.

NTFS deallocates sparse data streams and only maintains other data as allocated. When a program accesses a sparse file, the file system yields allocated data as actual data and deallocated data as zeros.

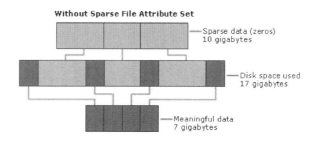

NTFS includes full sparse file support for both compressed and uncompressed files. NTFS handles read operations on sparse

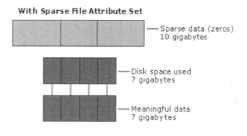

files by returning allocated data and sparse data. It is possible to read a sparse file as allocated data and a range of data without retrieving the entire data set, although NTFS returns the entire data set by default.

With the sparse file attribute set, the file system can deallocate data from anywhere in the file and, when an application calls, yield the zero data by range instead of storing and returning the actual data. File system application programming interfaces (APIs) allow for the file to be copied or backed as actual bits and sparse stream ranges. The net result is efficient file system storage and access. Next figure shows how data is stored with and without the sparse file attribute set.

For example, the properties of a file might show that the file is a 1-GB sparse file. Although the file is 1 GB, it occupies only 64 KB of disk space.

Journaling

NTFS is a journaling file system and uses the NTFS Log ($LogFile) to record metadata changes to the volume. It is a feature that FAT does not provide and critical for NTFS to ensure that its complex internal data structures will remain consistent in case of system crashes or data moves performed by the defragmentation API, and allow easy rollback of uncommitted changes to these critical data structures when the volume is remounted. Notably affected structures are the volume allocation bitmap, modifications to MFT records such as moves of some variable-length attributes stored in MFT records and attribute lists, and indices for directories and security descriptors.

The USN Journal (Update Sequence Number Journal) is a system management feature that records (in $Extend\$UsnJrnl) changes to files, streams and directories on the volume, as well as their various attributes and security settings. The journal is made available for applications to track changes to the volume.

Directory junctions

Junctions point are symbolic links to a directory that acts as an alias of that directory.
This feature offers benefits over a shortcut (.lnk) file, such as allowing access to files within the directory both via Windows Explorer and Command Prompt.

Unlike NTFS symbolic links, junction points can only link to a local volume; junction points from a local volume to a remote share are unsupported.

Hard links

The hard link feature allows different file names to directly refer to the same file contents. Hard links are similar to directory junctions, but refer to files instead.

Hard links may link only to files in the same volume, because each volume has its own MFT.

The NTFS file system has a limit of 1024 hard links on a file.

File compression

NTFS can compress files using LZNT1 algorithm.

Files are compressed in 16 cluster chunks (with 4 KB clusters, files are compressed in 64 KB chunks).

The compression algorithms in NTFS are designed to support cluster sizes of up to 4 KB: when the cluster size is greater than 4 KB on an NTFS volume, NTFS compression is not available.

If the compression reduces 64 KB of data to 60 KB or less, NTFS treats the unneeded 4 KB pages like empty sparse file clusters—they are not written.

This allows for reasonable random-access times as the OS just has to follow the chain of fragments. However, large compressible files become highly fragmented since every chunk smaller than 64 KB becomes a fragment.

Compression works best with files that have repetitive content, are seldom written, are usually accessed sequentially, and are not themselves compressed. Log files are an ideal example.

If system files that are needed at boot time (such as drivers, NTLDR, winload.exe, or BOOTMGR) are compressed, the system may fail to boot correctly, because decompression filters are not yet loaded.

Files may be compressed or decompressed individually (via changing the advanced attributes) for a drive, directory, or directory tree, becoming a default for the files inside.

References

- http://www.forensicswiki.org/wiki/New_Technology_File_Syste m_(NTFS)
- https://github.com/libyal/libfsntfs/blob/master/documentation /New%20Technologies%20File%20System%20(NTFS).asciidoc
- https://msdn.microsoft.com/en-us/library/dn365326.aspx

Volume Shadow Copies

Shadow Copy (also known as **Volume Snapshot Service, Volume Shadow Copy Service** or **VSS**) is a technology included in Microsoft Windows that allows taking manual or automatic backup copies or snapshots of computer files or volumes, even when they are in use.

It is implemented as a Windows service called the *Volume Shadow Copy* service and requires the file system to be NTFS in order to create and store shadow copies: Shadow Copies can be created on local and external volumes by any Windows component that uses this technology.

Overview

VSS operates at the block level of volumes.

A **snapshot** is a read-only point-in-time copy of the volume that allows the creation of consistent backups of a volume, ensuring that the contents do not change and are not locked while the backup is being made.

The core component of shadow copy is the **Volume Shadow Copy service**, which initiates and oversees the snapshot creation process, performing all necessary data transfers using components called *providers*.
Windows comes with a default **System Provider**, but software and hardware vendors can create their own software or hardware providers and register them with **Volume Shadow Copy service**.

Other components that are involved in the snapshot creation process are *writers*, used for aim of **Shadow Copy** is to create consistent reliable snapshots or to complete a series of inter-related changes to several related files.

Each writer is application-specific and has 60 seconds to establish a backup-safe state before providers start snapshot creation. If the **Volume Shadow Copy service** does not receive acknowledgement of success from the corresponding writers with this time-frame, it fails the operation.

Initially snapshots are temporary, they do not survive a reboot: the ability to create persistent snapshots was added in **Windows Server 2003** onward.

The end result is similar to a versioning file system, allowing any file to be retrieved as it existed at the time any of the snapshots was made.

Windows Versions

Windows XP and Server 2003

Volume Snapshot Service was first added to **Microsoft Windows** in **Windows XP**. It can only create temporary snapshots, used for accessing stable on-disk version of files that are opened for editing (and therefore locked).
This version of VSS is used by **NTBackup**.

The creation of persistent snapshots (which remain available across reboots until specifically deleted) has been added in **Windows Server 2003**, allowing up to 512 snapshots to exist simultaneously for the same volume.
In Windows Server 2003, **VSS** is used to create incremental periodic snapshots of data of changed files over time.

Its client component is included with Windows XP SP2 or later, and is available for installation on **Windows 2000 SP3** or later, as well as **Windows XP RTM** or SP1.

Windows XP and later include a command line utility called *vssadmin* that can list, create or delete volume shadow copies and list installed shadow copy writers and providers.

Windows Vista, 7 and Server 2008

Backup and **Restore** in **Windows Vista, Windows Server 2008, Windows 7** and **Windows Server 2008 R2** use shadow copies of files in both file-based and sector-by-sector backup.

The *System Protection* component uses VSS when creating and maintaining periodic copies of system and user data on the same local volume (similar to the Shadow Copies for Shared Folders feature in Windows Server) and allows reverting to an entire previous set of shadow copies called a *restore point*.
Furthermore, the *Previous Versions* feature in Windows Explorer allows restoring individual files or folders locally from restore points as they existed at the time of the snapshot.
Finally, **Windows Server 2008** introduces the diskshadow utility which exposes VSS functionality through 20 different commands.

The system creates shadow copies automatically once per day, or when triggered by the backup utility or installer applications which create a restore point.

Windows 8 and Server 2012

Windows 8 supports persistent shadow copies but lacks the GUI portion necessary to browse them: the ability to browse, search or recover older versions of files via the *Previous Versions* tab of the *Properties* dialog of files was removed for local volumes.

That functionality can be recovered using third party tools, such as **ShadowExplorer**.

The feature is fully available in **Windows Server 2012**.

Windows 10

Windows 10 restored the Previous Versions tab that was removed in **Windows 8**. However, it depends on the *File History* feature now instead of **Volume Shadow copy**.

Compatibility

While the different **NTFS** versions have a certain degree of both forward and backward compatibility, there are certain issues when mounting newer **NTFS** volumes containing persistent shadow copies in older versions of Windows.

This happens because the older operating system does not understand the newer format of persistent shadow copies.

Shadow Volume Copies in Digital Forensics
(Only NTFS)

Why Shadow Copies are important to Forensics

Windows Shadow Volumes can provide additional data that otherwise would not be available.

They can allow a forensic investigator to recover deleted files, and to learn what was taking place on a system before he/she began the investigation.

They are an excellent tool for discovering data that was previously deleted by a system user.

Limitations of Shadow Copies in forensic investigations

Although Shadow Copies can provide forensic investigators with files that have been deleted between the time the Shadow Copy was made and the time the investigation began, they only provide one previous version of files.

If previous changes to files were made before the Shadow Copy was created, those changes will not be known.

Because Shadow Copies clone on a block-level rather than a file-level, changes to individual files may not be enough to cause Windows to make the changes in a corresponding Shadow Copy.

Additionally, the *Shadow Copy service* might be turned off by the user, resulting in no **Shadow Copies** being stored.

Other times, the disk space settings might be set too low for multiple Shadow Copies to be saved, or even for one Shadow Copy to be saved if it is larger than what the settings allow.

Furthermore, Windows automatically overwrites Shadow Copies when the disk space limit is reached, so Shadow Copies should be an aid in a forensic investigation, but they are not guaranteed as a means to discover useful information.

Volume Shadow Copies in the Registry

We can also recover information about our Volume Shadow Copies, and their characteristics, from the Windows Registry. There are multiple locations of interest, especially as this is a Windows service.

The following registry key provides information on the service itself:

HKEY_LOCAL_MACHINE\SYSTEM\CurrentControlSet\Services\VSS

But the following registry key:

HKEY_LOCAL_MACHINE\SYSTEM\CurrentControlSet\Control\BackupRestore

contains three subkeys:

- **FilesNotToBackup** — specifies files that should not be backed up or restored.

Name	Type	Data
(Default)	REG_SZ	(value not set)
BITS_BAK	REG_MULTI_SZ	C:\WINDOWS\System32\Bits.bak
BITS_LOG	REG_MULTI_SZ	C:\WINDOWS\System32\Bits.log
BITS_metadata	REG_MULTI_SZ	C:\ProgramData\Microsoft\Network\Downloader*
ETW	REG_MULTI_SZ	%SystemRoot%\system32\LogFiles\WMI\RtBacku...
FVE_Control	REG_MULTI_SZ	\System Volume Information\FVE.{e40ad34d-dae9...
FVE_Log	REG_MULTI_SZ	\System Volume Information\FVE.{c9ca54a3-6983-...
FVE_Wipe	REG_MULTI_SZ	\System Volume Information\FVE.{9ef82dfa-1239-...
FVE2_Control	REG_MULTI_SZ	\System Volume Information\FVE2.{e40ad34d-dae...
FVE2_Log	REG_MULTI_SZ	\System Volume Information\FVE2.{c9ca54a3-698...
FVE2_VBB	REG_MULTI_SZ	\System Volume Information\FVE2.{24e6f0ae-6a00...
FVE2_Wipe	REG_MULTI_SZ	\System Volume Information\FVE2.{9ef82dfa-1239...
FVE2_WipeInfo	REG_MULTI_SZ	\System Volume Information\FVE2.{aff97bac-a69b...
FVE2_WipeX	REG_MULTI_SZ	\System Volume Information\FVE2.{9ef82dfa-1239...
Internet Explorer	REG_MULTI_SZ	%UserProfile%\index.dat /s
Kernel Dumps	REG_MULTI_SZ	%systemroot%\Minidump* /s %systemroot%\m...
Memory Page File	REG_MULTI_SZ	\Pagefile.sys
Mount Manager	REG_MULTI_SZ	\System Volume Information\MountPointManage...
MS Distributed Transaction Coordinator	REG_MULTI_SZ	C:\Windows\system32\MSDtc\MSDTC.LOG C:\Wi...
Netlogon	REG_MULTI_SZ	%SystemRoot%\netlogon.chg
Power Management	REG_MULTI_SZ	\hiberfil.sys
Storage Tiers Management	REG_MULTI_SZ	\System Volume Information\Heat*.* /s
Temporary Files	REG_MULTI_SZ	%TEMP%* /s
VSS Default Provider	REG_MULTI_SZ	\System Volume Information*{3808876B-C176-4e...
VSS Service Alternate DB	REG_MULTI_SZ	\System Volume Information*.{7cc467ef-6865-48...
VSS Service DB	REG_MULTI_SZ	\System Volume Information*.{7cc467ef-6865-48...
WER	REG_MULTI_SZ	%ProgramData%\Microsoft\Windows\WER* /s
WUA	REG_MULTI_SZ	%windir%\softwaredistribution*.* /s

- **FilesNotToSnapshot** (only Vista/2008+)— Specify files that should be deleted from newly-created shadow copies

Name	Type	Data
(Default)	REG_SZ	(value not set)
FVE	REG_MULTI_SZ	$AllVolumes$\System Volume Information\FVE
FVE2_Wipe	REG_MULTI_SZ	$AllVolumes$\System Volume Information\FVE
FVE2_WipeX	REG_MULTI_SZ	$AllVolumes$\System Volume Information\FVE
ModernOutlookOAB	REG_MULTI_SZ	$UserProfile$\AppData\Local\Packages\Micros
ModernOutlookOST	REG_MULTI_SZ	$UserProfile$\AppData\Local\Packages\Micros
OfficeODC	REG_MULTI_SZ	$UserProfile$\AppData\Local\Microsoft\Office
OutlookOAB	REG_MULTI_SZ	$UserProfile$\AppData\Local\Microsoft\Outlo
OutlookOST	REG_MULTI_SZ	$UserProfile$\AppData\Local\Microsoft\Outlo
Storage Tiers Management	REG_MULTI_SZ	\System Volume Information\Heat*.* /s
WUA	REG_MULTI_SZ	%windir%\softwaredistribution*.* /s

- **KeysNotToRestore** — Provides the names of registry keys and values that backup applications should not restore.

Name	Type	Data
(Default)	REG_SZ	(value not set)
Mount Manager	REG_MULTI_SZ	MountedDevices\
MS Distributed Transaction Coordinator	REG_MULTI_SZ	CurrentControlSet\Control\MSDTC\ASR\
Pending Rename Operations	REG_MULTI_SZ	CurrentControlSet\Control\Session Manager\PendingFileRenameOperatic
Pending Rename Operations2	REG_MULTI_SZ	CurrentControlSet\Control\Session Manager\PendingFileRenameOperatic
Session Manager	REG_MULTI_SZ	CurrentControlSet\Control\Session Manager\AllowProtectedRenames

If you ever find any discrepancies on a system that you are analyzing, I'd recommend pulling these registry keys and determining if there was a configuration change that altered data within a VSC.

Analyzing Volume Shadow Copies

When incorporating VSCs into your analysis, consider the following possibilities:

- When using tools such as libvshadow, that can give you a representation of the Volume Shadow Copy as a logical volume, you can apply secondary-analysis tools such as log2timeline/Plaso, and create massive, MEGA supertimelines that peek further back in history. Just note you might have an excess of the same data; use tools to de-dupe and you'll be in a good spot.

- If you have indicators to assist in analysis, such as malware or timeframes of interest, observe how your volume shadow copies interact with these timeframes. You may find yourself in a situation where you can peek at the system *prior* to infection. Additionally, if you have suspicions of timestomp, see if your Volume Shadow Copies back up that theory.
- Just because data is within a Volume Shadow Copy, it doesn't mean analysis techniques have to change. We can still run automated scripts, hash files, perform keyword searches, etc. This is just another data source!

Notes

*The identifier **3808876bc176-4e48-b7ae-04046e6cc752** is associated with **VSS** and would appear in any shadow copy on computers with VSS enabled.*

"The volume shadow service (VSS) runs once per day on a schedule. Its purpose is to compare the differences between 16KB blocks of data on the disk. If the data has changed from one day to the next, the block will be copied to the volume shadow copy file. The VSS does not perform multiple or incremental backups of data throughout the day."

References

- https://technet.microsoft.com/it-it/library/ee923636(v=ws.10).aspx
- http://www.forensicswiki.org/wiki/Windows_Shadow_Volumes
- https://en.wikipedia.org/wiki/Shadow_Copy
- https://msdn.microsoft.com/en-us/library/windows/desktop/bb891959(v=vs.85).aspx#filesnottobackup
- https://medium.com/@mbromileyDFIR/windows-wednesday-volume-shadow-copies-d20b60997c22

MAC(b) Times

The **MAC(b)** times are derived from file system metadata and they stand for:

- **M**odified (file content)
- **A**ccessed (file accessing)
- **C**hanged ($MFT Metadata Modified - es. **Permissions** or **ownership**)
- **B**irth (file creation time, not in FAT)

The (b) is in parentheses because not all file systems record a birth time.

Where are they stored?
Into two attributes, $STANDARD_INFO and $FILE_NAME:

$STANDARD_INFO
$STANDARD_INFO ($SI) stores file metadata such as flags, the file SID, the file owner and a set of MAC(b) timestamps.

$STANDARD_INFO is the timestamp collected by Windows explorer, fls, mactime, timestomp, find and the other utilities related to the display of timestamps.

$FILE_NAME
The $File_Name attribute contains forensically interesting bits, such as MACB times, file name, file length and more.

Timestamps are only updated with the attribute is changed. Files can have either one or two $File_Name attributes depending on how long the file name is. Short file names ("file.txt") has only one $File_Name attribute.

Long file names ("extremelylongfilename.txt") will have two $File_Name attributes.
One for the long file name, and one for the DOS-compatible short name (EXTRE~1.TXT).

What are the differences?

$STANDARD_INFO can be modified by user level processes like timestomp.
$FILE_NAME can only be modified by the system kernel. (*There are no known anti-forensics utilities that can accomplish this.*)

Time Rules

There are general rules when it comes to files being moved, copied, accessed or created.

Each operation alters different metadata, here a table of time rules related to **$STANDARD_INFORMATION**:

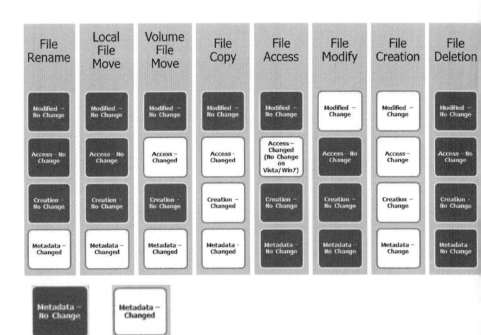

No Change   Change

While examining the **$FILENAME** timestamps the rules are pretty different:

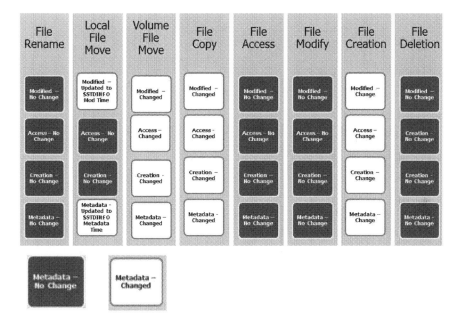

No Change   Change

How to detect Anti-Forensics Timestamp Anomalies?

Tool such as **timestomp** allow attackers to backdate a file to an arbitrary time in order to trying to hide it in system32 or other similar directories.

So, during analysis you can use analyzeMFT.py in order to **check if the $FILENAME time occurs after the $STANDARD_INFORMATION Creation Time**.

If this anomaly occurs, it is likely that an attacker has been alterated timestamps in **$STANDARD_INFO** using timestomp.

$FILENAME Creation Time >
$STANDARD_INFORMATION Creation Time =
Timestomp activity

Memory analysis

Volatility

The Volatility Framework is collection of tools, implemented in Python under the GNU General Public License, for the extraction of digital artifacts from volatile memory (RAM) samples.

The extraction techniques are performed completely independent of the system being investigated but offer visibility into the runtime state of the system.

Volatility Plugins reference

Plugin	Description
amcache	Print AmCache information
apihooks	Detect API hooks in process and kernel memory
apihooksdeep	Detect API hooks in process and kernel memory, with ssdeep for whitelisting
atoms	Print session and window station atom tables
atomscan	Pool scanner for atom tables
attributeht	Find Hacking Team implants and attempt to attribute them using a watermark.
auditpol	Prints out the Audit Policies from HKLM\SECURITY\Policy\PolAdtEv
autoruns	Searches the registry and memory space for applications running at system startup and maps them to running processes
bigpools	Dump the big page pools using BigPagePoolScanner
bioskbd	Reads the keyboard buffer from Real Mode memory
cachedump	Dumps cached domain hashes from memory
callbacks	Print system-wide notification routines
chromecookies	Scans for and parses potential Chrome cookie data

chromedownlo adchains	Scans for and parses potential Chrome download chain records
chromedownlo ads	Scans for and parses potential Chrome download records
chromehistory	Scans for and parses potential Chrome url history
chromesearchte rms	Scans for and parses potential Chrome keyword search terms
chromevisits	Scans for and parses potential Chrome url visits data -- VERY SLOW, see -Q option
clipboard	Extract the contents of the windows clipboard
cmdline	Display process command-line arguments
cmdscan	Extract command history by scanning for _COMMAND_HISTORY
connections	Print list of open connections [Windows XP and 2003 Only]
connscan	Pool scanner for tcp connections
consoles	Extract command history by scanning for _CONSOLE_INFORMATION
crashinfo	Dump crash-dump information
deskscan	Poolscaner for tagDESKTOP (desktops)
devicetree	Show device tree
dlldump	Dump DLLs from a process address space
dlllist	Print list of loaded dlls for each process
driverbl	Scans memory for driver objects and compares the results with the baseline image
driverirp	Driver IRP hook detection
driveritem	
drivermodule	Associate driver objects to kernel modules
driverscan	Pool scanner for driver objects
dumpcerts	Dump RSA private and public SSL keys
dumpfiles	Extract memory mapped and cached files
dumpregistry	Dumps registry files out to disk
editbox	Displays information about Edit controls. (Listbox experimental.)
envars	Display process environment variables
eventhooks	Print details on windows event hooks
evtlogs	Extract Windows Event Logs (XP/2003 only)

fileitem	
filescan	Pool scanner for file objects
firefoxcookies	Scans for and parses potential Firefox cookies (cookies.sqlite moz_cookies table
firefoxdownloads	Scans for and parses potential Firefox download records -- downloads.sqlite moz_downloads table pre FF26 only
firefoxhistory	Scans for and parses potential Firefox url history (places.sqlite moz_places table)
gahti	Dump the USER handle type information
gditimers	Print installed GDI timers and callbacks
gdt	Display Global Descriptor Table
getservicesids	Get the names of services in the Registry and return Calculated SID
getsids	Print the SIDs owning each process
handles	Print list of open handles for each process
hashdump	Dumps passwords hashes (LM/NTLM) from memory
hibinfo	Dump hibernation file information
hivedump	Prints out a hive
hivelist	Print list of registry hives.
hivescan	Pool scanner for registry hives
hookitem	
hpakextract	Extract physical memory from an HPAK file
hpakinfo	Info on an HPAK file
idt	Display Interrupt Descriptor Table
idxparser	Scans for and parses Java IDX files
iehistory	Reconstruct Internet Explorer cache / history
imagecopy	Copies a physical address space out as a raw DD image
imageinfo	Identify information for the image
impscan	Scan for calls to imported functions
joblinks	Print process job link information
kdbgscan	Search for and dump potential KDBG values
kpcrscan	Search for and dump potential KPCR values
ldrmodules	Detect unlinked DLLs
lsadump	Dump (decrypted) LSA secrets from the registry

machoinfo	Dump Mach-O file format information
malfind	Find hidden and injected code. *Volatility's malfind plugin scans memory looking for sections marked as executable with no associated mapped file on disk and files in the Microsoft Portable Executable (PE) format.*
malfinddeep	Find hidden and injected code, whitelist with ssdeep hashes
malprocfind	Finds malicious processes based on discrepancies from observed, normal behavior and properties
malsysproc	Find malware hiding in plain sight as system processes
mbrparser	Scans for and parses potential Master Boot Records (MBRs)
memdump	Dump the addressable memory for a process
memmap	Print the memory map
messagehooks	List desktop and thread window message hooks
mftparser	Scans for and parses potential MFT entries
mimikatz	mimikatz offline
moddump	Dump a kernel driver to an executable file sample
modscan	Pool scanner for kernel modules
modules	Print list of loaded modules
multiscan	Scan for various objects at once
mutantscan	Pool scanner for mutex objects
ndispktscan	Extract the packets from memory
notepad	List currently displayed notepad text
objtypescan	Scan for Windows object type objects
openioc_scan	Scan OpenIOC 1.1 based indicators
openvpn	Extract OpenVPN client credentials (username, password) cached in memory.
patcher	Patches memory based on page scans
poolpeek	Configurable pool scanner plugin
prefetchparser	Scans for and parses potential Prefetch files
printkey	Print a registry key, and its subkeys and values
privs	Display process privileges
procdump	Dump a process to an executable file sample
processbl	Scans memory for processes and loaded DLLs and compares the results with the baseline

pslist	Print all running processes by following the EPROCESS lists
psscan	Pool scanner for process objects
pstotal	Combination of pslist,psscan & pstree --output=dot gives graphical representation
pstree	Print process list as a tree
psxview	Find hidden processes with various process listings
qemuinfo	Dump Qemu information
raw2dmp	Converts a physical memory sample to a windbg crash dump
registryitem	
rsakey	Extract base64/PEM encoded private RSA keys from physical memory.
schtasks	Scans for and parses potential Scheduled Task (.JOB) files
screenshot	Save a pseudo-screenshot based on GDI windows
servicebl	Scans memory for service objects and compares the results with the baseline image
servicediff	List Windows services (ala Plugx)
serviceitem	
sessions	List details on _MM_SESSION_SPACE (user logon sessions)
shellbags	Prints ShellBags info
shimcache	Parses the Application Compatibility Shim Cache registry key
shimcachemem	Parses the Application Compatibility Shim Cache stored in kernel memory
shutdowntime	Print ShutdownTime of machine from registry
sockets	Print list of open sockets
sockscan	Pool scanner for tcp socket objects
ssdeepscan	Scan process or kernel memory with SSDeep signatures
ssdt	Display SSDT entries
strings	Match physical offsets to virtual addresses (may take a while, VERY verbose)
svcscan	Scan for Windows services
symlinkscan	Pool scanner for symlink objects
thrdscan	Pool scanner for thread objects
threads	Investigate _ETHREAD and _KTHREADs

timeliner	Creates a timeline from various artifacts in memory
timers	Print kernel timers and associated module DPCs
truecryptmaster	Recover TrueCrypt 7.1a Master Keys
truecryptpassphrase	TrueCrypt Cached Passphrase Finder
truecryptsummary	TrueCrypt Summary
trustrecords	Extract MS Office TrustRecords from the Registry
uninstallinfo	Extract installed software info from Uninstall registry key
unloadedmodules	Print list of unloaded modules
userassist	Print userassist registry keys and information
userhandles	Dump the USER handle tables
usnparser	Scans for and parses USN journal records
vaddump	Dumps out the vad sections to a file
vadinfo	Dump the VAD info
vadtree	Walk the VAD tree and display in tree format
vadwalk	Walk the VAD tree
vboxinfo	Dump virtualbox information
verinfo	Prints out the version information from PE images
vmwareinfo	Dump VMware VMSS/VMSN information
volshell	Shell in the memory image
windows	Print Desktop Windows (verbose details)
wintree	Print Z-Order Desktop Windows Tree
wndscan	Pool scanner for window stations
yarascan	Scan process or kernel memory with Yara signatures

Notes

Volatility interprets and parses the contents of volatile memory samples, such as system RAM, and provides details such as processes which were running on the system prior to acquisition. The tool does not modify data during analysis.

Volatility is an application which is used to examine RAM images. The tool does not collect the RAM images, there are separate tools which complete this task. Therefore so long as the examiner works on a read-only copy of the original preserved memory image there will not be any modifications or changes to the evidence. The tool does not examine RAM slack, this artifact is the data at the end of a file and before the end of the first sector prior. The data after RAM slack is called file slack and fills the remaining cluster allocated to the file.

External References

http://www.volatilityfoundation.org/

https://github.com/volatilityfoundation/volatility/wiki

Process Hollowing

Process hollowing is a technique used by malware in which a legitimate process is loaded on the system solely to act as a container for hostile code.

At launch, the legitimate process is created in a suspended state and the process's memory is replaced with the code of a second program so that the second program runs instead of the original program.

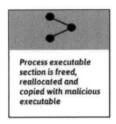

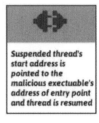

| *Malware Creates a legitimate process in the suspended state* | *Process executable section is freed, reallocated and copied with malicious executable* | *Suspended thread's start address is pointed to the malicious exectuable's address of entry point and thread is resumed* | *Used to disguise malware process as legitimate process* |

The advantage is that this helps the process hide amongst normal processes better: Windows and process monitoring tools believe the original process is running, whereas the actual program running is different.

Detecting hollowed processes with Volatility

One common technique for detecting hollowed processes is by scanning allocated memory for segments that have the RWX protection setting.
If the attacker forgot to fix memory protection flags with **VirtualProtectEx**, we can find it easily.

A Volatility plugin called 'malfind.py' does this as part of its scanning: however, careful malware authors can easily avoid this by correcting protection settings after they are done writing to memory.

But, using volatility without any plugins we can dump processes to files and compare them with eachother or with their original file on the filesystem.

Mitigation

Mitigating specific API calls will likely have unintended side effects, such as preventing legitimate software from operating properly.
So efforts should be focused on preventing adversary tools from running earlier in the chain of activity and on identifying subsequent malicious behavior.

Windows Registry

Persistence techniques

Windows Registry

Run/RunOnce Keys

Windows has a lot of AutoStart Extension Points(**ASEP**).
When it comes to malware, most of them would like to achieve persistence by editing the below registry keys at User Level:

HKEY_CURRENT_USER\Software\Microsoft\Windows\CurrentVersion\Run
HKEY_CURRENT_USER\Software\Microsoft\Windows\CurrentVersion\RunOnce

If the malware gains admin privileges, it can edit some keys at admin/system level privileges:

HKEY_LOCAL_MACHINE\SOFTWARE\Microsoft\Windows\CurrentVersion\Run
HKEY_LOCAL_MACHINE\SOFTWARE\Microsoft\Windows\CurrentVersion\RunOnce
HKEY_LOCAL_MACHINE\Software\Microsoft\Windows\CurrentVersion\Policies\Explorer\Run

BootExecute Key

Since **smss.exe** launches before windows subsystem loads, it calls configuration subsystem to load the hive present at

HKLM\SYSTEM\CurrentControlSet\Control\hivelist

Also smss.exe will launch anything present in the BootExecute key at

HKEY_LOCAL_MACHINE\SYSTEM\ControlSet002\Control\Session Manager

It should always have the value of autocheck autochk*. If there are more values in it, then probably the malware is likely to launch at boot.

Userinit Key

Winlogon process uses the value specified in the Userinit key to launch login scripts etc.

This key is location at

```
HKEY_LOCAL_MACHINE\SOFTWARE\Microsoft\Windows
NT\CurrentVersion\Winlogon
```

Usually, userinit key points to userinit.exe but if this key can be altered, then that exe will also launch by Winlogon.

Notify

Since Winlogon handles Secure Attention Sequence (SAS) (Ctrl+Alt+Del), notify subkeys found at

```
HKEY_LOCAL_MACHINE\SOFTWARE\Microsoft\Windows
NT\CurrentVersion\Winlogon\Notify
```

are used to notify event handles when SAS happens and loads a DLL. This DLL can be edited to launch whenever such SAS event occurs.

Explorer.exe

Pointed by key located at

```
HKEY_LOCAL_MACHINE\SOFTWARE\Microsoft\Windows
NT\CurrentVersion\Winlogon\Shell
```

this key points to **explorer.exe** and should only be string explorer.exe rather than complete path as it is supposed to launch from \windows.

The boot key at

```
HKEY_LOCAL_MACHINE\SOFTWARE\Microsoft\Windows
NT\CurrentVersion\IniFileMapping\system.ini\boot
```

points to the location under Winlogon only.

Startup Keys

Placing a malicious file under the startup directory is often used by malware authors.

Any shortcut created to the location pointed by subkey Startup will launch the service during logon/reboot.

Start up location is specified both at **Local Machine** and **Current User**.

HKEY_CURRENT_USER\Software\Microsoft\Windows\CurrentVersion\Explorer\User Shell Folders

HKEY_CURRENT_USER\Software\Microsoft\Windows\CurrentVersion\Explorer\Shell Folders

HKEY_LOCAL_MACHINE\SOFTWARE\Microsoft\Windows\CurrentVersion\Explorer\Shell Folders

HKEY_LOCAL_MACHINE\SOFTWARE\Microsoft\Windows\CurrentVersion\Explorer\User Shell Folders

Services

Many windows services are required to run at boot like **Workstation/server services**, **Windows Event Log**, and other Win drivers. These are located at

HKEY_LOCAL_MACHINE\SYSTEM\CurrentControlSet\services.

Along with placing a malicious file in the above-listed registry key, there is another way to load malicious files. Malicious files can be loaded if a service fails to start.

There are some other keys which are used to start background services like remote registry service. These are located at:

HKEY_LOCAL_MACHINE\Software\Microsoft\Windows\CurrentVersion\RunServices Once

HKEY_LOCAL_MACHINE\Software\Microsoft\Windows\CurrentVersion\RunServices

Browser Helper Objects

It is essentially a **DLL** module loaded when **Internet Explorer** starts up. Various data theft types malware affect **Browser Helper Objects**.

They are located at

HKEY_LOCAL_MACHINE\SOFTWARE\Microsoft\Windows\CurrentVersion\Explorer\Browser Helper Objects.

There are various subkeys under BHO which tell the browser to load which DLLs.

AppInit_DLLs

Key located at

```
HKEY_LOCAL_MACHINE\SOFTWARE\Microsoft\Windows
NT\CurrentVersion\Windows\AppInit_DLLs
```

will show the DLLs loaded by the **User32.dll**.

As most executables load **User32.dll**, this is a good place for malicious DLLs to reside.

File Association

There are various keys which are used to specify the action when a certain type of files are open, located at

```
HKEY_LOCAL_MACHINE\Software\Classes\

HKEY_CLASSES_ROOT\
```

Notes

- *Autoruns shows you what programs are configured to run during system bootup or login, and when you start various built-in Windows applications like Internet Explorer, Explorer and media players. These programs and drivers include ones in your startup folder, **Run, RunOnce**, and other Registry keys. **Autoruns** reports Explorer shell extensions, toolbars, browser helper objects, **Winlogon** notifications, auto-start services, and much more.*

- ***Autorunsc** is the command-line version of **Autoruns**. Its usage syntax is:*

Usage: autorunsc [-a <*|bdeghiklmoprsw>] [-c|-ct]
[-h] [-m] [-s] [-u] [-vt] [[-z] | [user]]]

DLL Search Order Hijacking

Another common method used by malware is to hijack a concept about how the OS loads DLLs. Whenever an exe loads (even **explorer.exe**), it follows a certain path search to load the required DLLs.

Because DLLs are loaded in the order the directories are parsed, it is possible to add a malicious DLL with the same name in a directory earlier than the directory where the legit DLL resides.

If Safe DLL search mode is enabled (which is by default on most versions) then OS will check whether the DLL is already loaded in memory or is it a part of Known DLLs registry key located at

HKEY_LOCAL_MACHINE\SYSTEM\CurrentControlSet\Control\Session Manager\KnownDLLs.

If OS cannot find the DLL at either of these, then DLL search starts in the following order

- Directory from where application was launched
- System Directory(\Windows\System32)
- Windows Directory
- Current Working Directory
- Directories defined in the PATH variable.

So a malware can easily place a malicious DLL in the search order.

Shortcut Hijacking

Simple but very effective technique: hijack the shortcut icons Target attribute. Along with a normal application to be launched, shortcut icon can be forced to download content from an evil site.

Note that there are various other methods like infecting **MBR**, **COM** object hijack, etc. are also by malware, but above are some of the common method used by malware to achieve persistence.

Bootkit

A bootkit is a malware variant that modifies the boot sectors of a hard drive, including the Master Boot Record (MBR) and Volume Boot Record (VBR).

Malicious programs may use bootkits to persist on systems at a layer below the operating system, which may make it difficult to perform full remediation unless an organization suspects one was used and can act accordingly.

Master Boot Record

The MBR is the section of disk that is first loaded after completing hardware initialization by the BIOS. It is the location of the boot loader. An adversary who has raw access to the boot drive may overwrite this area, diverting execution during startup from the normal boot loader to adversary code.

Volume Boot Record

The MBR passes control of the boot process to the VBR. Similar to the case of MBR, an adversary who has raw access to the boot drive may overwrite the VBR to divert execution during startup to adversary code.

COM Hijacking

The *Microsoft Component Object Model* (**COM**) is a system within Windows to enable interaction between software components through the operating system.

Malware can use this system to insert malicious code that can be executed in place of legitimate software through hijacking the **COM** references and relationships as a means for persistence.

Hijacking a **COM** object requires a change in the **Windows Registry** to replace a reference to a legitimate system component which may cause that component to not work when executed.

When that system component is executed through normal system operation the adversary's code will be executed instead.

Amcache and Shimcache

Amcache and **Shimcache** can provide a timeline of which program was executed and when it was first run and last modified. In addition, these artifacts provide program information regarding the file path, size, and hash depending on the OS version.

Amcache

The **Amcache.hve** file is a registry file that stores the information of executed applications.

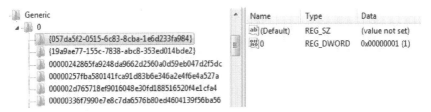

These executed applications include the execution path, first executed time, deleted time, and first installation.

On Windows 8, **Amcache.hve** replaces **RecentFileCache.bcf** and uses the **Windows NT Registry File** (REGF) format.

A common location for **Amcache.hve** is:

```
%SystemRoot%\AppCompat\Programs\Amcache.hve
```

Amcache.hve file is also an important artifact to record the traces of anti-forensic programs, portable programs, and external storage devices, and can be analyzed using the **amcache** plugin of **RegRipper** (https://github.com/keydet89/RegRipper2.8)

Shimcache

Shimcache, also known as **AppCompatCache**, is a component of the **Application Compatibility Database**, which was created by Microsoft and used by the Windows operating system to identify application compatibility issues.

This helps developers troubleshoot legacy functions and contains data related to Windows features.

It is used for quick search to decide whether modules need shimming for compatibility or not.

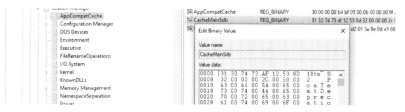

A Shim is a small library that transparently handles the applications interworking's to provide support for older APIs in a newer environment or vice-versa.

Shims allow backwards and forwards compatibility for applications on different software platforms.

The Registry Key related to this cache is located at

HKLM\SYSTEM\CurrentControlSet\Control\SessionManager\AppCompatCache\AppCompatCache

Forensic examiners can use indicators they find in the ShimCache data to triage other data sources, such as AmCache.hve file, Prefetch files with sources such as "Service Control Manager" in a timeline.

Shimcache can be investigated using **ShimCacheParser.py**, by Mandiant (https://github.com/mandiant/ShimCacheParser)

Notes

- **Amcache**: *FIRST* execution of a program
- **Shimcache/AppCompatCache**: execution of the *last version* of the program

> *The **AppCompatCache** or **ShimCache** is a windows registry key that records if an application was launched or accessed by Windows Explorer. The key records the data and time the file was last modified and can indicate if the application was*

launched by the user. ***It does not record the number of times, the parent process or user identification information.***

Recent opened Programs/Files/URLs

HKCU\Software\Microsoft\Windows\CurrentVersion\Explorer\ComDlg32\OpenSavemRU

MRU is the abbreviation for most-recently-used.

This key maintains a list of recently opened or saved files via Windows Explorer-style dialog boxes (**Open/Save** dialog box).
For instance, files (e.g. .txt, .pdf, htm, .jpg) that are recently opened or saved files from within a web browser are maintained.

Documents that are opened or saved via Microsoft Office programs are *not maintained*.

Whenever a new entry is added to **OpenSaveMRU (OpenSavePidIMRU since Vista)** key, registry value is created or updated in

HKCU\Software\Microsoft\Windows\CurrentVersion\Explorer\ComDlg32\LastVisitedMRU

This key correlates to the previous **OpenSaveMRU** key to provide extra information: each binary registry value under this key contains a recently used program executable filename, and the folder path of a file to which the program has been used to open or save it.

The list of files recently opened directly from **Windows Explorer** are stored into

HKCU\Software\Microsoft\Windows\CurrentVersion\Explorer\RecentDocs

This key corresponds to **%USERPROFILE%\Recent** (*My Recent Documents*) and contains local or network files that are recently opened and only the filename in binary form is stored.

Start>Run

The list of entries executed using the **Start>Run** command in mantained in this key:

```
HKCU\Software\Microsoft\Windows\CurrentVersion\Explorer\RunMRU
```

If a file is executed via **Run** command, it will leaves traces in the previous two keys **OpenSaveMRU** and **RecentDocs**.

Deleting the subkeys in RunMRU does not remove the history list in Run command box immediately.

By using Windows "Recent Opened Documents" Clear List feature via **Control Panel>Taskbar and Start Menu**, an attacker can remove the Run command history list.

In fact, executing the Clear List function will remove the following registry keys and their subkeys:

```
HKCU\Software\Microsoft\Windows\CurrentVersion\Explorer\RecentDocs\
HKCU\Software\Microsoft\Windows\CurrentVersion\Explorer\RunMRU\
HKCU\Software\Microsoft\Internet Explorer\TypedURLs\
HKCU\Software\Microsoft\Windows\CurrentVersion\Explorer\ComDlg32\OpenSav
eMRU
HKCU\Software\Microsoft\Windows\CurrentVersion\Explorer\ComDlg32\LastVisite
dMRU
```

UserAssist

```
HKCU\Software\Microsoft\Windows\CurrentVersion\Explorer\UserAssist
```

This key contains two **GUID** subkeys: each subkey maintains a list of system objects such as program, shortcut, and control panel applets that a user has accessed.

The UserAssist registry key tracks GUI-based programs executed from the desktop.

Registry values under these subkeys are weakly encrypted using **ROT-13** algorithm which basically substitutes a character with another character 13 position away from it in the ASCII table.

ROT13 reference

Char	ROT13	Char	ROT13
a	N	n	A
b	O	o	B
c	P	p	C
d	Q	q	D
e	R	r	E
f	S	s	F
g	T	t	G
h	U	u	H
i	V	v	I
j	W	w	J
k	X	x	K
l	Y	y	L
m	Z	z	M

```
.exe = .RKR
.lnk = .YAX
```

Shell bag

Microsoft Windows uses a set of Registry keys known as "shellbags" to maintain the size, view, icon, and position of a folder when using Explorer.

Shell bag entries reflect folder access, not program execution.

- On a Windows XP system, shellbags may be found under:

```
HKEY\_USERS\{USERID}\Software\Microsoft\Windows\Shell\
HKEY\_USERS\{USERID}\Software\Microsoft\Windows\ShellNoRoam\
```

The NTUser.dat hive file persists the Registry key HKEY_USERS\{USERID}\.

- On a Windows 7 system, shellbags may be found under:

```
HEKY\_USERS\{USERID}\Local Settings\Software\Microsoft\Windows\Shell\
```

The UsrClass.dat hive file persists the registry key HKEY_USERS\{USERID}\.

Recent URLs

```
HKCU\Software\Microsoft\Internet Explorer\TypedURLs
```

This key contains a listing of 25 recent URLs (or file path) that is typed in the **Internet Explorer** (IE) or **Windows Explorer** address bar: the key will only show links that are fully typed, automatically completed while typing, or links that are selected from the list of stored URLs in IE address bar.

Websites that are accessed via IE Favorites are not recorded, and if the user clears the URL history using Clear History via IE Internet Options menu, this key will be completely removed.

Notes

OpenSavePIDlMRU: The location that stores the values for the files that have been recently opened on a Windows 7 host. These files are arranged by extension in the key.

LastVisitedPiDMRU: indicates the application that launched the file.

The **prefetch** files indicate files that are loaded by the system to increase performance.

The **thumbs.db** file does not exist at this location for Window 7, it is a Windows XP artifact.

Installed programs

All programs listed in **Control Panel>Add/Remove Programs** correspond to one subkey into this key:

```
HKLM\SOFTWARE\Microsoft\Windows\CurrentVersion\Uninstall
```

Subkeys usually contains these two common registry values:

- **DisplayName** — program name

- **UninstallString** — application Uninstall component's file path, which indirectly refers to application installation path

Other possible useful registry values may exist, which include information on install date, install source and application version.

Windows Protect Storage

Protected Storage is a service used by **Microsoft** products to provide a secure area to store private information.

Information that could be stored in **Protected Storage** includes for example **Internet Explorer** AutoComplete strings and passwords, **Microsoft Outlook** and **Outlook Express** accounts' passwords.

Windows Protected Storage is maintained under this key:

HKCU\Software\Microsoft\Protected Storage System Provider

Registry Editor hides these registry keys from users viewing, including administrator.

Pagefile

HKLM\SYSTEM\CurrentControlSet\Control\Session Manager\Memory Management

This key maintains the configuration of Windows virtual memory: the paging file (usually **C:\pagefile.sys**) may contain evidential information that could be removed once the suspect computer is shutdown.

This key contains a registry value called **ClearPagefileAtShutdown** which specify whether Windows should clear off the paging file when the computer shutdowns (*by default, windows will not clear the paging file*).

During a forensic analysis you should check this value before shutting down a suspect computer!

Windows Search

HKCU\Software\Microsoft\Search Assistant\ACMru

This key contains recent search terms using Windows default search.

There may be up to four subkeys:

- **5001**: Contains list of terms used for the Internet Search Assistant

- **5603**: Contains the list of terms used for the Windows files and folders search

- **5604**: Contains list of terms used in the "word or phrase in a file" search

- **5647**: Contains list of terms used in the "for computers or people" search

Notes

*Search terms entered in the Windows 7 Start menu bar are recorded in the **WordWheelQuery** registry key.*

File extensions

This key contains instruction to execute any .exe extension file:

```
HKCR\exefile\shell\open\command\
```

Normally, this key contains one default value with data "%1" %*, but if the value's data is changed to something similar to somefilename.exe "%1" %* , investigator should suspect some other hidden program is invoked automatically when the actual .exe file is executed.

Malware normally modify this value to load itself covertly

This technique apply to other similar keys, including:

```
HKEY_CLASSES_ROOT\batfile\shell\open\command
HKEY_CLASSES_ROOT\comfile\shell\open\command
```

Mounted drives

The list of mounted devices, with associated persistent volume name and unique internal identifier for respective devices is contained into

```
HKLM\SYSTEM\MountedDevices
```

This key lists any volume that is mounted and assigned a drive letter, including **USB** storage devices and external **DVD/CDROM** drives.

From the listed registry values, value's name that starts with "\DosDevices\" and ends with the associated drive letter, contains information regarding that particular mounted device.

Similar informations are contained also in

```
HKCU\Software\Microsoft\Windows\CurrentVersion\Explorer\MountPoints2\CPC\V olume\
```

which is located under the respective device **GUID** subkey and in the binary registry value named Data.

This key is a point of interest during a forensic analysis: the key records shares on remote systems such **C$**, **Temp$**, etc.

The existence of ProcDump indicates the dumping of credentials within lsass.exe address space. Sc.exe indicates the adding of persistence such as Run keys or services. The presence of .rar files may indicate data exfiltration.

The history of recent mapped network drives is store into

```
HKCU\Software\Microsoft\Windows\CurrentVersion\Explorer\Map Network Drive MRU
```

In addition, permanent subkey (unless manually removed from registry) regarding mapped network drive is also created in

```
HKCU\Software\Microsoft\Windows\CurrentVersion\Explorer\MountPoints2
```

and the subkey is named in the form of **##servername#sharedfolder**.

USB Storage

The key:

```
HKLM\SYSTEM\CurrentControlSet\Enum\USBSTOR
```

contains addition information about list of mounted **USB** storage devices, including external memory cards.

When used in conjunction with two previous keys will provide evidential information.

Debugging

This key allows administrator to map an executable filename to a different debugger source, allowing user to debug a program using a different program:

```
HKLM\SOFTWARE\Microsoft\Windows NT\CurrentVersion\Image File Execution Options\
```

Modification to this key requires administrative privilege.

This feature could be exploited to launch a completely different program under the cover of the initial program.

Windows Events

Event log files provide digital forensic practitioners with a wealth of data describing the operations of computer systems: they often contain valuable information that could connect particular user events or activities to specific times.

Windows event logs provide a range of descriptors to allow for the compilation of events into categories from "informational" to "critical."

Individual event IDs indicate specific types of events and recent Windows versions have separate event log files for various applications and services.

Structure and location

Depending on the version of Windows installed on the system under investigation, the number and types of events will differ.

In fact, the events logged by a **Windows XP** machine may be incompatible with an event log analysis tool designed for Windows 8.

For example, **Event ID 551** on a **Windows XP** machine refers to a logoff event; the Windows Vista/7/8 equivalent is **Event ID 4647**.

Windows XP events can be converted to Vista events by adding 4096 to the Event ID.

Windows versions since Vista include a number of new events that are not logged by Windows XP systems. Windows Server editions have larger numbers and types of events.

Thus, the exact version of the Windows system must be considered very carefully when developing a digital forensic process centered on event logs.

By default, a Windows system is set to log a limited number of events, but it can be modified to include actions such as file deletions and changes.

The default locations of Windows event logs are typically

Windows 2000/Server2003/Windows XP:

```
%SystemRoot%\System32\Config\*.evt
```

Windows Vista/7/Server2008:

```
%SystemRoot%\System32\winevt\Logs\*.evtx
```

This can be changed by a user by modifying the File value of the following registry keys in **HKEY LOCAL MACHINE (HKLM)** on the local machine:

- **Application Events**:
  HKLM\SYSTEM\CurrentControlSet\services\eventlog\Application
- **Hardware Events:**
  HKLN\SYSTEM\CurrentControlSet\services\eventlog\HardwareEvents
- **Security Events:** HKLM\SYSTEM\CurrentControlSet\services
  \eventlog\Security
- **System Events:** HKLM\SYSTEM\CurrentControlSet\services
  \eventlog\System

When a custom path is used, a key is generated at the registry location:

```
HKLM\Microsoft\Windows\CurrentVersion\WINEVT\Channels\[logname]
```

(e.g., Microsoft-Windows-Audio\CaptureMonitor)

Useful events for forensics analysis

Event ID (2000/XP/2003)	Event ID (Vista/7/8/2008/2012)	Description	Log Name
528	4624	Successful Logon	Security

529	4625	Failed Login	Security
680	4776	Successful /Failed Account Authentication	Security
624	4720	A user account was created	Security
636	4732	A member was added to a security-enabled local group	Security
632	4728	A member was added to a security-enabled global group	Security
2934	7030	Service Creation Errors	System
2944	7040	The start type of the IPSEC Services service was changed from disabled to auto start.	System
2949	7045	Service Creation	System

Logon Type Codes

One of the useful information that Successful/Failed Logon event provide is how the user/process tried to logon (Logon Type) but Windows display this information as a number and here is a list of the logon type and their explanation:

Logon type	Logon title	Description

2	Interactive	A user logged on to this computer.
3	Network	A user or computer logged on to this computer from the network.
4	Batch	Batch logon type is used by batch servers, where processes may be executing on behalf of a user without their direct intervention.
5	Service	A service was started by the Service Control Manager.
7	Unlock	This workstation was unlocked.
8	NetworkCleartext	A user logged on to this computer from the network. The user's password was passed to the authentication package in its unhashed form. The built-in authentication packages all hash credentials before sending them across the network. The credentials do not traverse the network in plaintext (also called cleartext).
9	NewCredentials	A caller cloned its current token and specified new credentials for outbound connections. The new logon session has the same local identity, but uses different credentials for other network connections.
10	RemoteInteractive	A user logged on to this computer remotely using Terminal Services or Remote Desktop.
11	CachedInteractive	A user logged on to this computer with network credentials that were stored locally on the computer. The domain controller was not contacted to verify the credentials.

Security Identifiers (SIDs)

A **Security Identifier** (commonly abbreviated **SID**) is a unique, immutable identifier of a user, user group, or other security principal. A security principal has a single SID for life (in a given domain), and all properties of the principal, including its name, are associated with the SID.

This design allows a principal to be renamed (for example, from "Jane Smith" to "Jane Doe") without affecting the security attributes of objects that refer to the principal.

The SID is variable in length and encapsulates the hierarchical notion of issuer and identifier. It consists of a 6-byte *identifier authority* field that is followed by one to fourteen 32-bit *subauthority* values and ends in a single 32-bit *relative identifier(RID)*.

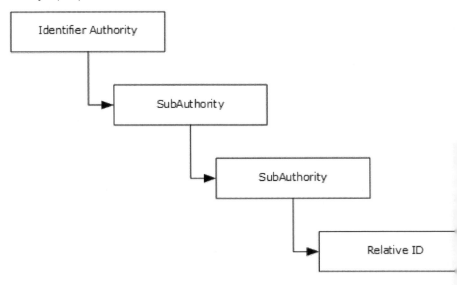

When displayed textually, the accepted form is the following:

S-1-<identifier authority>-<sub1>-<sub2>-...-<subn>-<rid>

where *S* and *1* are literal strings, *identifier authority* is the 6-byte value, *sub1* through *subn* are the subauthority values, and *rid* is the RID.

RID is a **Relative IDentifier**. Relative to the **SID** that is. The **RID** is the last part and should be unique for a certain object within a domain.

> *Windows allocates RIDs starting at 1,000; RIDs having a value less than 1,000 are considered reserved and are used for special accounts.*

> **For example, all Windows accounts with a RID of 500 are considered built-in Administrator accounts in their respective issuing authorities.**

So, the format of a SID can be illustrated using the following example:

"S-1-5-21-3623811015-3361044348-30300820-1013"

1	5	21-3623811015-3361044348-30300820	1013
The version of the SID specification	The identifier authority value	Domain or local computer identifier	The Relative ID (RID)

Machine SIDs

The machine SID is stored in the **SECURITY** registry hive located at **SECURITY\SAM\Domains\Account**, this key has two values **F** and **V**.

The **V** value is a binary value that has the computer SID embedded within it at the end of its data (last 96 bits).

- "NewSID ensures that this SID is in a standard NT 4.0 format (3 32-bit subauthorities preceded by three 32-bit authority fields). Next, NewSID generates a new random SID for the computer. NewSID's generation takes great pains to create a truly random 96-bit value, which replaces the 96-bits of the 3 subauthority values that make up a computer SID."

Decoding Machine SID

The SID number is used in file, registry, service and users permissions.
The machine SID is determined in hexadecimal form from here:

- regedit.exe: **\HKEY_LOCAL_MACHINE\SAM\SAM\Domains\Account\V** (last 12 bytes)

- explorer.exe: **\%windir%\system32\config\SAM**

If the SAM file is missing at startup, a backup is retrieved in hexadecimal form here:

- regedit.exe: **\HKEY_LOCAL_MACHINE\SECURITY\Policy\PolAcDmS\@** (last 12 bytes)

- explorer.exe: **\%windir%\system32\config\SECURITY**

Example	2E,43,AC,40,C0,85,38,5D,07,E5,3B,2B
1) Divide the bytes into 3 sections:	2E,43,AC,40 - C0,85,38,5D - 07,E5,3B,2B
2) Reverse the order of bytes in each section:	40,AC,43,2E - 5D,38,85,C0 - 2B,3B,E5,07
3) Convert each section into decimal:	1085031214 - 1563985344 - 725345543
4) Add the machine SID prefix:	S-1-5-21-1085031214-1563985344-725345543

Service SIDs

Service SIDs are a feature of service isolation, a security feature introduced in Windows Vista and Windows Server 2008.

Service isolation lets administrators control what local resources (e.g., files, registry keys on the local machine) a Windows service can access.
Any service with the "unrestricted" SID-type property will have a service-specific SID added to the access token of the service host process.

The purpose of Service SIDs is to allow permissions for a single service to be managed without necessitating the creation of service accounts, an administrative overhead.

Each service SID is a local, machine-level SID generated from the service name using the following formula:

```
S-1-5-80-{SHA-1(service name in upper case)}
```

The sc.exe utility can be used to generate an arbitrary service SID:

```
C:\>sc.exe showsid dnscache

NAME: dnscache
SERVICE SID: S-1-5-80-859482183-879914841-863379149-1145462774-
2388618682
STATUS: Active
```

The service can also be referred to as NT SERVICE\<service_name> (e.g. "NT SERVICE\dnscache").

Well-known security identifiers

SID	RID	Description
S-1	0	NULL SID authority: used to hold the "null" account SID
S-1-0	0	The null account
S-1	1	World SID authority: used for the "Everyone" group, which is the only account in this authority.
S-1-1	0	The Everyone group (\EVERYONE)
S-1	2	Local SID authority: used for the "Local" group, which is the only account in this group.
S-1-2	0	The Local group
S-1	3	Creator SID authority: responsible for the CREATOR_OWNER, CREATOR_GROUP, CREATOR_OWNER_SERVER and CREATOR_GROUP_SERVER well known SIDs. These SIDs are used as placeholders in an access control list (ACL) and are replaced by the user, group, and machine SIDs of the security principal.
S-1-3	0	Creator Owner account (\CREATOR OWNER)
S-1-3	1	Creator Group account (\CREATOR GROUP)
S-1-3	2	Creator Owner Server account (\CREATOR SERVER OWNER)
S-1-3	3	Creator Group Server account (\CREATOR SERVER GROUP)
S-1	4	Non-unique authority: Not used by NT
S-1	5	NT authority: accounts that are managed by the NT security subsystem.
S-1-5	2	NT authority: Network (AUTHORITY\NETWORK)
S-1-5	4	NT authority: Interactive (AUTHORITY\INTERACTIVE)
S-1-5	11	NT authority: Authenicated users (AUTHORITY\AUTHENTICATED USERS)

S-1-5	18	NT authority: System (AUTHORITY\SYSTEM)
S-1-5	19	NT authority: Local service (AUTHORITY\LOCAL SERVICE)
S-1-5	20	NT authority: Network service (AUTHORITY\NETWORK SERVICE)
S-1-5	21	Non-unique SIDs, used for domain SIDs: The SID S-1-5-21 is followed by 3 RIDs (96 bytes) that defines the domain. Which could look like this S-1-5-21-0123456789-0123456789-0123456789. The 3 RIDs are created during initial domain installation. Since it is a random number duplicates can exist, there is no such thing as a central domain number authority. The domain SID is followed by a RID identifying the account within the domain. This RID is just a simple counter assigning a new RID to an account. There are however a couple well known RIDs:

RID	Name	Type
500	DOMAINNAME\Administrator	User
501	DOMAINNAME\Guest	User
512	DOMAINNAME\Domain Admins	Group
513	DOMAINNAME\Domain Users	Group
514	DOMAINNAME\Domain Guests	Group

S-1-5	32	Builtin resources:		
		RID	**Name**	**Type**
		544	BUILTIN\Administrators	Group
		545	BUILTIN\Users	Group
		546	BUILTIN\Groups	Group
		548	BUILTIN\Account Operators	Group
		549	BUILTIN\Server Operators	Group
		550	BUILTIN\Print Operators	Group
		551	BUILTIN\Backup Operators	Group
		552	BUILTIN\Replicator	Group
S-1	9	Resource manager authority: is a catch-all that is used for 3rd party resource managers.		

Forensics Tools

Sleuthkit

A collection of command line tools that allows you to analyze disk images and recover files from them.

Tool	Description
fsstat	Shows file system details and statistics including layout, sizes, and labels.
ffind	Finds allocated and unallocated file names that point to a given meta data structure.
fls	Lists allocated and deleted file names in a directory. It will process the contents of a given directory and can display information on deleted files. (output: body file)
icat	Extracts the data units of a file, which is specified by its meta data address (instead of the file name).
ifind	Finds the meta data structure that has a given file name pointing to it or the meta data structure that points to a given data unit.
ils	Lists the meta data structures and their contents in a pipe delimited format. (output: body file)
istat	Displays the statistics and details about a given meta data structure in an easy to read format.
blkcat	Extracts the contents of a given data unit.
blkls	Lists the details about data units and can extract the unallocated space of the file system.
blkstat	Displays the statistics about a given data unit in an easy to read format.
blkcalc	Calculates where data in the unallocated space image (from blkls) exists in the original image. This is used when evidence is found in unallocated space.
jcat	Display the contents of a specific journal block.
jls	List the entries in the file system journal.

img_stat	tool will show the details of the image format
img_cat	This tool will show the raw contents of an image file.
disk_stat	This tool will show if an HPA exists.
hfind	Uses a binary sort algorithm to lookup hashes in the NIST NSRL, Hashkeeper, and custom hash databases created by md5sum.
mactime	Takes input from the fls and ils tools (body file) to create a timeline of file activity.
sorter	Sorts files based on their file type and performs extension checking and hash database lookups. It runs the 'file' command on each file and organizes the files according to the rules in configuration files. Extension mismatching is also done to identify 'hidden' files. One can also provide hash databases for files that are known to be good and can be ignored and files that are known to be bad and should be alerted.
sigfind	Searches for a binary value at a given offset. Useful for recovering lost data structures.

https://www.sleuthkit.org/

DensityScout

This tool calculates density (like entropy) for files of any file-system-path to finally output an accordingly descending ordered list, with the **lowest and most suspect values** at the top.

https://www.cert.at/downloads/software/densityscout_en.html

Plaso

Tool designed to extract timestamps from various files found on a typical computer systems and aggregate them.

Plaso is a Python-based backend engine for the tool log2timeline.

Tool	Description
image_export	Export file content from a storage media image or device based on various filter criteria, such as extension names, filter paths, file format signature identifiers, file creation date and time ranges, etc.
log2timeline	Extract events from individual files, recursing a directory (e.g. mount point) or storage media image or device. log2timeline creates a plaso storage file which can be analyzed with the pinfo and psort tools. The plaso storage file contains the extracted events and various metadata about the collection process alongside information collected from the source data. It may also contain information about tags applied to events and reports from analysis plugins.
pinfo	Provide information (metadata) about the contents of a plaso storage file. (output Body File)
psort	Post-process plaso storage files. It allows you to filter, sort and run automatic analysis on the contents of plaso storage files. *psort's "time slice" capability allows just the events near a pivot point to be viewed*
plasm (deprecated)	Tags events based on criteria (*groups and tags events in a Plaso storage file*)

https://github.com/log2timeline/plaso/wiki

Foremost

Console program to recover files based on their headers, footers, and internal data structures: can work on image files, such as those generated by dd, Safeback, Encase, etc, or directly on a drive.

The headers and footers can be specified by a configuration file or you can use command line switches to specify built-in file types. These built-in types look at the data structures of a given file format allowing for a more reliable and faster recovery.

```
foremost version 1.5.7 by Jesse Kornblum, Kris Kendall, and Nick Mikus.
$ foremost [-v|-V|-h|-T|-Q|-q|-a|-w-d] [-t <type>] [-s <blocks>] [-k <size>]
      [-b <size>] [-c <file>] [-o <dir>] [-i <file]

-V  - display copyright information and exit
-t  - specify file type.  (-t jpeg,pdf ...)
-d  - turn on indirect block detection (for UNIX file-systems)
-i  - specify input file (default is stdin)
-a  - Write all headers, perform no error detection (corrupted files)
-w  - Only write the audit file, do not write any detected files to the disk
-o  - set output directory (defaults to output)
-c  - set configuration file to use (defaults to foremost.conf)
-q  - enables quick mode. Search are performed on 512 byte boundaries.
-Q  - enables quiet mode. Suppress output messages.
-v  - verbose mode. Logs all messages to screen
```

http://foremost.sourceforge.net/

md5deep

A set tools to compute hashes, or message digests, for any number of files while optionally recursively digging through the directory structure. It can also take a list of known hashes and display the filenames of input files whose hashes either do or do not match any of the known hashes.

```
$ md5deep [OPTION]... [FILES]...
See the man page or README.txt file or use -hh for the full list of options
-p <size> - piecewise mode. Files are broken into blocks for hashing
-r        - recursive mode. All subdirectories are traversed
-e        - show estimated time remaining for each file
-s        - silent mode. Suppress all error messages
-z        - display file size before hash
-m <file> - enables matching mode. See README/man page
-x <file> - enables negative matching mode. See README/man page
-M and -X are the same as -m and -x but also print hashes of each file
-w        - displays which known file generated a match
-n        - displays known hashes that did not match any input files
-a and -A add a single hash to the positive or negative matching set
-b        - prints only the bare name of files; all path information is omitted
-l        - print relative paths for filenames
-t        - print GMT timestamp (ctime)
-i/I <size> - only process files smaller/larger than SIZE
-v        - display version number and exit
-d        - output in DFXML; -u - Escape Unicode; -W FILE - write to FILE.
-j <num>  - use num threads (default 48)
-Z - triage mode;   -h - help;   -hh - full help
```

https://github.com/jessek/hashdeep/

RegRipper

Tool for getting data quickly out of the windows registry: it produces reports based upon pre-canned registry searches. using plugins to extract information out of the registry files. Each plugin has been created to handle a specific kind of data stored in the registry keys.

```
Rip v.2.8_20130801 - CLI RegRipper tool
Rip [-r Reg hive file] [-f plugin file] [-p plugin module] [-l] [-h]
Parse Windows Registry files, using either a single module, or a plugins file.


  -r Reg hive file...Registry hive file to parse
  -g ................Guess the hive file (experimental)
  -f [profile].......use the plugin file (default: plugins\plugins)
  -p plugin module...use only this module
  -l ................list all plugins
  -c ................Output list in CSV format (use with -l)
  -s system name.....Server name (TLN support)
  -u username........User name (TLN support)
  -h.................Help (print this information)


Ex: C:\>rip -r c:\case\system -f system
   C:\>rip -r c:\case\ntuser.dat -p userassist
   C:\>rip -l -c


All output goes to STDOUT; use redirection (ie, > or >>) to output to a file.


copyright 2013 Quantum Analytics Research, LLC
```

https://github.com/keydet89/RegRipper2.8

Log Parser

Tool that provides universal query access to text-based data such as log files, XML files and CSV files, as well as key data sources on the Windows operating system such as the Event Log, the Registry, the file system, and Active Directory

https://www.microsoft.com/en-us/download/details.aspx?id=24659

python-evtx

Python parser for recent Windows Event Log files (.evtx).

```
usage: evtx_dump.py [-h] evtx


Dump a binary EVTX file into XML.


positional arguments:
  evtx       Path to the Windows EVTX event log file


optional arguments:
  -h, --help  show this help message and exit
```

http://www.williballenthin.com/evtx/

EvtxParser

A parser framework for Microsoft Windows Vista event log files in their native binary (.evtx) format.

http://computer.forensikblog.de/en/2011/11/evtx-parser-1-1-1.html

Hibr2Bin

Hibernation File Decompressor: allows users to uncompress Windows hibernation file, like volatility's **hibinfo** plugin.

```
Hibr2Bin 3.0

Copyright (C) 2007 - 2017, Matthieu Suiche <http://www.msuiche.net>

Copyright (C) 2012 - 2014, MoonSols Limited <http://www.moonsols.com>

Copyright (C) 2015 - 2017, Comae Technologies FZE <http://www.comae.io>


Usage: Hibr2Bin [Options] /INPUT <FILENAME> /OUTPUT <FILENAME>


Description:

Enables users to uncompress Windows hibernation file.


Options:

    /PLATFORM, /P        Select platform (X64 or X86)

    /MAJOR, /V           Select major version (e.g. 6 for NT 6.1

    /MINOR, /M           Select minor version (e.g. 1 for NT 6.1)

    /OFFSET, /L          Data offset in hexadecimal (optional)

    /INPUT, /I           Input hiberfil.sys file.

    /OUTPUT, /O          Output hiberfil.sys file.


Versions:

    /MAJOR 5 /MINOR 1     Windows XP

    /MAJOR 5 /MINOR 2     Windows XP x64, Windows 2003 R2

    /MAJOR 6 /MINOR 0     Windows Vista, Windows Server 2008

    /MAJOR 6 /MINOR 1     Windows 7, Windows Server 2008 R2

    /MAJOR 6 /MINOR 2     Windows 8, Windows Server 2012

    /MAJOR 6 /MINOR 3     Windows 8.1, Windows Server 2012 R2

    /MAJOR 10 /MINOR 0    Windows 10, Windows Server 2016
```

Uncompress a Windows 7 (NT 6.1) x64 hibernation file:

HIBR2BIN /PLATFORM X64 /MAJOR 6 /MINOR 1 /INPUT hiberfil.sys /OUTPUT uncompressed.bin

Uncompress a Windows 10 (NT 10.0) x86 hibernation file:

HIBR2BIN /PLATFORM X86 /MAJOR 10 /MINOR 0 /INPUT hiberfil.sys /OUTPUT uncompressed.bin

https://github.com/comaeio/Hibr2Bin

Kansa

PowerShell scripts to run on remote hosts and copy over applications to collect foresic information (included autorun programs).

https://github.com/davehull/Kansa

Sigcheck

Command-line utility that shows file version number, timestamp information, and digital signature details, including certificate chains. It also includes an option to check a file's status on VirusTotal, a site that performs automated file scanning against over 40 antivirus engines, and an option to upload a file for scanning.

https://docs.microsoft.com/en-us/sysinternals/downloads/sigcheck

PECmd

Tool for analyzing a system's prefetch files.

https://github.com/EricZimmerman/PECmd

ShimCacheParser

Tool for reading the Application Compatibility Shim Cache stored in the Windows registry. Metadata of files that are executed on a Windows system are placed within this data structure on the running system.

The ShimCacheParser python script was used to produce this list of artifacts. All applications when run on a current version of Windows will be checked and logged in the AppCompatCache registry key regardless of whether they need to be shimmed or run with different environmental variables. Permissions and boot time launch are not recorded by this key.

---

usage: ShimCacheParser.py [-h] [-v] [-t] [-B] [-o FILE]

[-l | -b BIN | -m XML | -z ZIP | -i HIVE | -r REG]

Parses Application Compatibilty Shim Cache data

optional arguments:

  -h, --help   show this help message and exit

  -v, --verbose   Toggles verbose output

  -t, --isotime   Use YYYY-MM-DD ISO format instead of MM/DD/YY default

  -B, --bom   Write UTF8 BOM to CSV for easier Excel 2007+ import

  -l, --local   Reads data from local system

  -b BIN, --bin BIN   Reads data from a binary BIN file

  -m XML, --mir XML   Reads data from a MIR XML file

  -z ZIP, --zip ZIP   Reads ZIP file containing MIR registry acquisitions

  -i HIVE, --hive HIVE Reads data from a registry reg HIVE

  -r REG, --reg REG   Reads data from a .reg registry export file

  -o FILE, --out FILE Writes to CSV data to FILE (default is STDOUT)

---

https://github.com/mandiant/ShimCacheParser

Forensic Workflows

The chain of custody

In forensic scope, the "chain of custody" refers to

The chronological documentation or paper trail that records the sequence of custody, control, transfer, analysis, and disposition of physical or electronic evidence.

Particularly important in criminal cases, the concept is also applied in civil litigation—and sometimes more broadly in drug testing of athletes, and in supply chain management, e.g. to improve the traceability of food products, or to provide assurances that wood products originate from sustainably managed forests.

In a digital forensic context, digital evidences are different from physical evidence, in that a carefully protected image of a hard drive is as valid as the original hard drive in the eyes of a court: the first image of a hard drive that investigators take is known as the "best evidence," because it's closest to the original source.

At this "best evidence" must be attached a chain of custody form and both should be stored under lock and key.

The Chain of Custody Form

To prove chain of custody, you'll need a form that details how the evidence was handled every step of the way.

The form should answer these questions:

- What is the evidence?
  For example: hardware information (photos, description, serial number, asset ID, hostname) and digital information (filename, md5 hash)
- How did you get it?
  Information about used tools, type of acquisition (live or offline), storage format
- When was it collected?
- Who has handled it?
- Why did that person handle it?
- Where was it stored?
  Information about the physical location in which the proof is stored, or information (model/SN/IP) of the storage/NAS used to store the forensic image.

The CoC Form must be keep up-to-date: every single time the best evidence is handed off, the chain of custody form needs to be updated.

Furthermore, if the best evidence is duplicated, an hashing process should be performed on both digital copies, in order to prove that the evidence you started with is the same as the evidence you ended up with.

Every forensic investigator could be develop his own Chain-Of-Custody form.

In my case, was useful this template provided by NIST:

https://www.nist.gov/sites/default/files/documents/2017/04/28/Sample-Chain-of-Custody-Form.docx

Description of Evidence		
Item #	Quantity	Description of Item (Model, Serial #, Condition, Marks, Scratches)

Chain of Custody				
Item #	Date/Time	Released by (Signature & ID#)	Received by (Signature & ID#)	Comments/Location

Memory acquisition

One of the first steps that you need to perform when you deal with the forensic analysis of a compromised machine is to make a copy of volatile memory.

But, which tool should be used to make the acquisition of volatile memory?

Below my own shortlist.

DumpIt
DumpIt is a fusion of two trusted tools, **win32dd** and **win64dd**, combined into one one executable.
Simply double-click the DumpIt executable and allow the tool to run: the snapshot of the host's physical memory will be taken and saved into the folder where the executable was located.

This tool is a part of the Community edition of MoonSols Windows Memory Toolkit.

Image creation process

1. Create a command prompt utilizing the local admin account of the target system and connect an external USB media to the device on which DumpIT will be in.

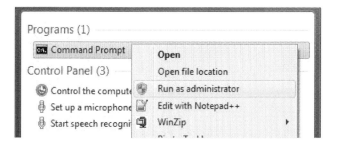

2. Navigate to the location where DumpIT is stored within the external HDD. Ensure that the external USB media has enough storage to store the memory.

3. Run DumpIT :

```
E:\>DumpIT.exe /Q /T RAW /N
```

This will create a raw memory dump within the working directory that was used to start the dumpit executable. Successful execution will result in raw dump and a json file with metadata.

The files will utilize the following naming convention:

```
<hostname>-<YYYYMMDD>-<HHMMSS>.dmp
<hostname>-<YYYYMMDD>-<HHMMSS>.json.
```

The screenshot below shows a successful creation of a memory dump.

FTK Imager

Can acquire live memory and paging file on 32bit and 64bit systems.
Runs on **Windows 2003** and later versions

http://accessdata.com/support/adownloads#FTKImager

Image creation process

1. Login to via local admin account on the target system.

2. Connect the external **HDD** into the target system.

5. Open Windows Explorer and navigate to the **FTK Imager Lite** folder within the external **HDD**.

6. Run **FTK Imager.exe** as an administrator (*right click -> Run as administrator*).

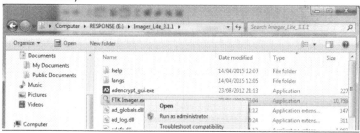

7. In FTK's main window, go to **File** and click on **Capture Memory**.

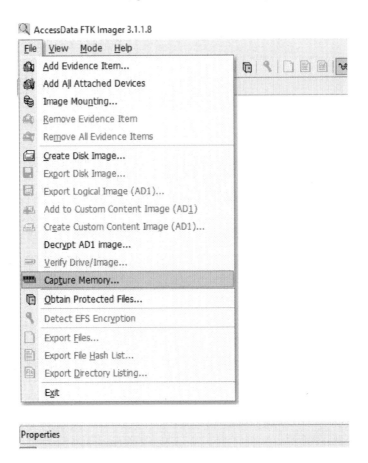

8. In the *Destination Path* browse for the correct collection folder, choose a filename according to naming policy and (optionally) select the *Include pagefile* checkbox. Finally click **OK**.

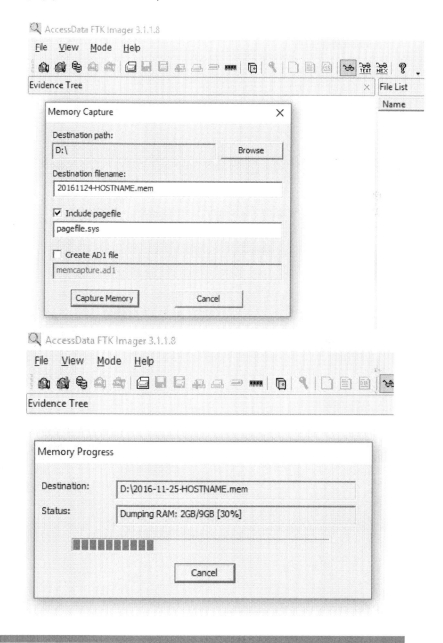

WinPmem

Part of **Rekall Memory Analysis framework.**

It supports **Windows XP** to **Windows 8**, both 32 and 64 bit architectures.

Image creation process

Go to https://github.com/google/rekall/releases folder, download the correct version of WinPmem.exe and put it on the External HDD:

1. Select **winpmem-2.1.post4.exe** for windows system above Windows 2008
2. Select **winpmem_1.6.2.exe** for windows systems below Windows 2008
2. Create a command prompt utilizing the local admin account of the target system and connect an external USB/HDD to the device which WinPmem executable will be in.

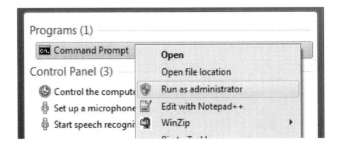

3. Navigate to the location where **WinPmem** is stored within the external HDD. Ensure that the external USB media has enough storage to store the memory dump.

4. Run **WinPmem** (please log the date, time and command used)

   1. If using winpmem-2.1.post4.exe, follow the below command:

```
E:\> winpmem-2.1.post4.exe –o <destination path filename.aff4>
```

   2. If using winpmem_1.6.2.exe, follow the below command:

```
E:\> winpmem_1.6.2.exe <destination path filename.aff4>
```

5. At the end of the collection, the **winpmem** driver will be unloaded automatically.

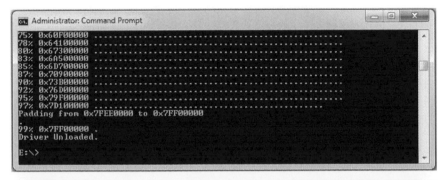

Disk acquisition

FTK Imager

The *Forensic Toolkit Imager* (**FTK Imager**) is a commercial forensic imaging software package distributed by **AccessData**.

It comes in 2 versions: GUI version, and Command-Line only.

GUI: http://accessdata.com/product-download/ftk-imager-lite-version-3.1.1

Command Line: http://accessdata.com/product-download/windows-32bit-3.1.1

CAINE (Computer Aided INvestigative Environment)
GNU/Linux live distribution that offers a complete forensic environment organized to integrate existing software tools as software modules and to provide a friendly graphical interface.

Download: http://www.caine-live.net/

Image acquisition on a running system

Using FTK Imager (on 64 bit Windows Systems)

3. Login to via local admin account on the target system.

4. Connect the external **HDD** into the target system.

5. Take notes on the information about the affected system: computer name and system characteristics. This can be found at: Start -> Computer -> Properties.
   NOTE: Take a screenshot and put it on the external HDD.

4. Identify and take notes on the volumes that are currently mounted on the system through the Computer Management console (*Start -> right click on Computer -> Manage*). Navigate into *"Disk Management"*.

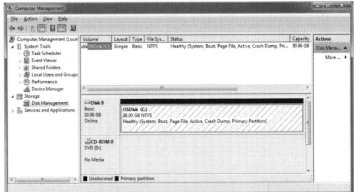

NOTE: Take a screenshot and put it screenshot on the external HDD

9. Open Windows Explorer and navigate to the **FTK Imager Lite** folder within the external **HDD**.

10. Run **FTK Imager.exe** as an administrator (*right click -> Run as administrator*).

11. In FTK's main window, go to **File** and click on **Create Disk Image**.

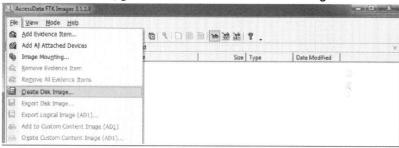

12. Select *Physical Drive* as the source evidence type. Click on **Next**.

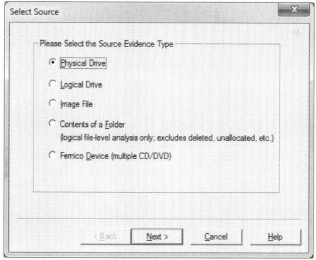

9. Select the actual physical drive from the drop down list and click on **Finish**.

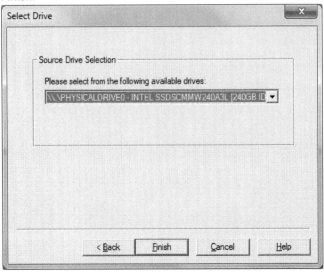

10. In the *Create Image* window click on **Add** (in the *Image Destination(s)* section).

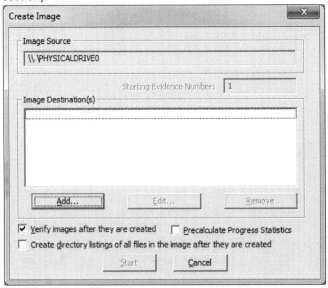

11. Select *E01* as the destination image type and click on **Next**.

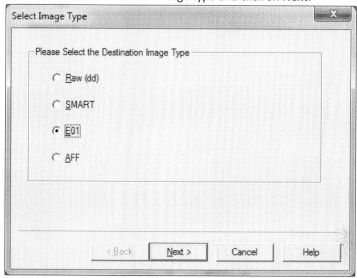

12. Complete the Evidence Item Information and click **Next**. Here an example:

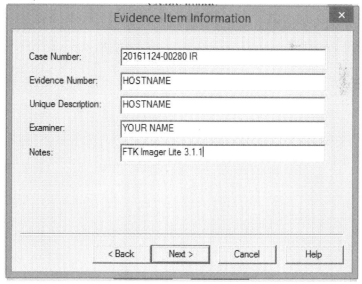

13. In the *Image Destination Folder* browse for the external collection drive (if different from the response drive) and click **OK**.

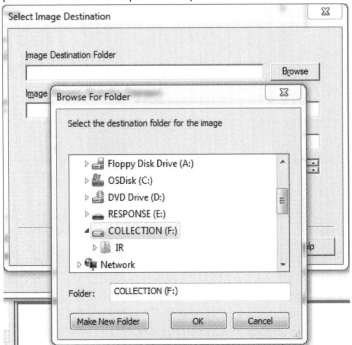

14. Provide a name for the image within the *Image Filename* box. Usually I use this naming convention: **DATE_TIME_HOSTNAME**. (Example: **08122016_1500_WEB001**)

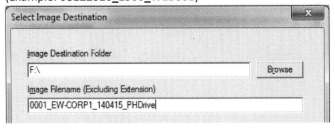

15. Change the *Image Fragment* to 2048. Additionally, set the level of compression to 9 (smallest). Click on **Finish**.

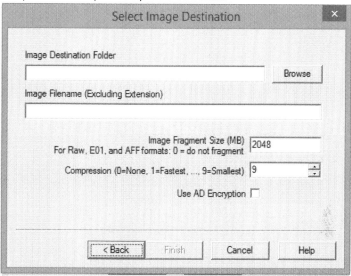

16. Check *"Precalculate Progress Statistics"* to see how much time and storage space creating the custom image will require before you start.

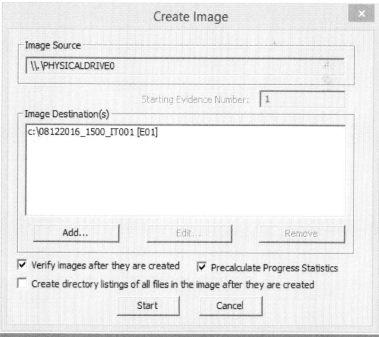

17. Click on **Start** and record the time in your notes.

The progress of the imaging process will be displayed as well as the elapsed and remaining time.

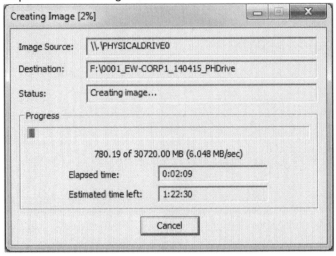

18. If the option *"Verify images after they are created"* was selected in step 16, the verification process starts immediately after the imaging process finishes.

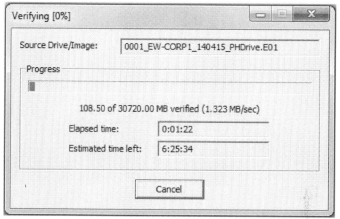

The verification process might take some time to complete, but do not cancel it as it is important to know if the image was successfully created.

19. After the image is generated, a log file is created in the same location where the image is saved.

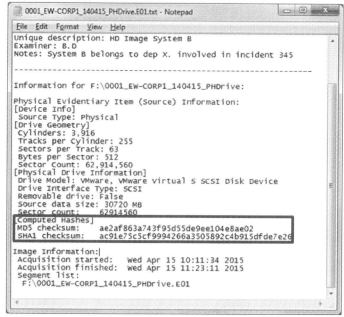

Using command line FTK Imager (for 32 bit Windows System)

If you are trying to image 32 bit Windows System, you will need to use **FTK Imager Command Line**:

1. Login **with a local admin account** on the target system.

2. Connect the external **HDD** into the target system that has **FTK Imager Command Line** folder residing on it.

3. Take notes on the information about the affected system: computer name and system characteristics. This can be found at: **Start -> Computer -> Properties**.
    NOTE: Take a screenshot and put it screenshot on the external HDD.

4. Identify and take notes on the volumes that are currently mounted on the system through the Computer Management console (**Start -> right-click on Computer -> Manage**). Navigate into '**Disk Management**'.

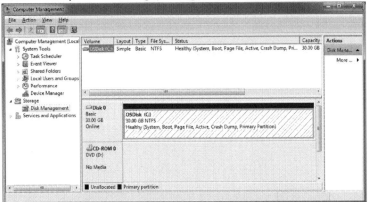

NOTE: Take a screenshot and put it screenshot on the external HDD

5. Open a command prompt

6. Navigate to the location of the **FTK Imager Command Line** Folder and then run the following command:

```
E:\>ftkimager.exe <HARD DRIVE THAT YOU WANT TO IMAGE> e:\<Destination
path of output file with name NOT extension> --e01 --frag 2G -compress 9 -
verify
```

Example:

```
E:\>ftkimager.exe \\.\PhysicalDrive0 e:\IMAGE_FOLDER\filename --e01 --frag
2G --compress 9 --verify
```

You should be seeing the following type of information:

```
AccessData FTK Imager v3.1.1 CLI (Aug 20 2012)
Copyright 2006-2012 AccessData Corp., 384 South 400 West, Lindon, UT 84042
All rights reserved.

Creating image...
1278.13 / 488386.34 MB (116.19 MB/sec) - 1:09:52 left
```

Image acquisition on a powered off system

1. Start the system with a **Live linux distribution** from CD or USB Stick:
    Ubuntu, **Kali** or (my suggestion) **CAINE**.

2. Connect the external **HDD** into the target system.

3. Mount the file system by creating a mount point and then mounting the
    external disk (ex. */dev/sdb1*).

```
root@caine:~# mkdir /mnt/target
root@caine:~# mount /dev/sdb1 /mnt/target
```

4. Create a cryptographic fingerprint of the original disk (ex. */dev/sda*)
    using **MD5**. This will be used to verify the integrity of the duplicate.

```
root@caine:~# md5sum /dev/sda > /mnt/target/08122016_1500_WEB001.md5
```

5. Use dd with the input source being the /dev/sda and the output file with chosen name.
    (Example: **08122016_1500_WEB001**)
    Other useful options is the **conv=sync,noerror** to avoid stopping the image creation when founding an unreadable sector.
    If such sector is found with this option, it will skip over the unreadable section (noerror) and pad the output (sync).

```
root@caine:~#dd if=/dev/sda of=/mnt/target/08122016_1500_WEB001.img
conv=sync,noerror bs=8k

19536363+0 records in

19536363+0 records out

160041885696 bytes (160 GB) copied, 5669.92 s, 28.2 MB/s
```

6. Finally create the fingerprint of the image created and verify that both fingerprints match and unmount the drive.

```
root@caine:~#md5sum /mnt/target/08122016_1500_WEB001.img >
/mnt/target/08122016_1500_WEB001.img.md5
root@caine:~# cat /mnt/target/*.md5

6a5346b9425925ed230e32c9a0b510f7  /mnt/target/08122016_1500_WEB001.im
g
6a5346b9425925ed230e32c9a0b510f7  /dev/sda

root@caine:~# umount /mnt/target/
```

Image acquisition over the network

In some occasions you need to acquire an image of a computer using a boot disk and network connectivity.

Usually, this approach is made with a Linux boot disk on the machine under analysis, and another computer used as imaging collection platform, connected via a network hub or through a crossover cable.

The reasons this approach could be related to level of physical access to the hardware or interface issues to local resources: for example, you might come across a machine that has a drive interface that is incompatible with your equipment and without USB port.

Where possible, I suggest to use a crossover cable, in order to ensure security and integrity of the data.

The setup

In order to accomplish imaging across the network, we will need to setup a collection box to "listen" for data from target box. We do this using netcat.

Once you have the target computer booted with a **Linux Boot CD** you'll need to ensure the two computers are configured on the same network, and can communicate.

So, once the two boxes are connected with a cross cable, you need to configure the network, using the ifconfig command.

On the acquisition box:

```
ifconfig eth0 192.168.0.1 netmask 255.255.255.0
```

or using **ip** command:

```
ip address add 192.168.0.1/24 dev eth0
```

And on the target machine:

```
ifconfig eth0 192.168.0.2 netmask 255.255.255.0
```

or using **ip**:

```
ip address add 192.168.0.2/24 dev eth0
```

The acquisition

Now that we have both computers talking, we can start the imaging process. First check the hash of the subject disk:

```
sha1sum /dev/sda
```

Then, the next step is to open a "listening" port on the acquisition computer. We will do this with netcat (in this case we are using an external USB drive mounted on **/mnt/evidences**):

```
nc -l -p 8888 | dd of=/mnt/evidences/forensic_image.raw
```

The command opens a listening session (**-l**) on TCP port **8888** (**-p 8888**) and pipes any traffic that comes across that port to the **dd** command which writes the datastream on **/mnt/evidences/forensic_image.dd**.

Then, on the target computer we issue the dd command: instead of giving the command an output file parameter using **of=**, we pipe the **dd** command output to **netcat** and send it to our listening port (**8888**) on the acquisition computer at IP address **192.166.0.1**:

```
dd if=/dev/sda | nc 192.168.0.1 8888
```

Finally, after we receive our completion messages from **dd** on both boxes (*records in / records out*), we can kill the **nc** listening on the acquisition box with a simple *ctrl+c*.

This should return to prompt on both sides of the connections.

You should check both the hash of the physical disk that was imaged on the target computer and the resulting image on the acquisition box to see if they match:

```
sha1sum /mnt/evidence/forensic_image.raw
```

If the hashes match, the acquisition was successful.

Timeline creation

Sleutkit

Sleuth Kit is a collection of command line tools that allows you to analyze disk images.

https://www.sleuthkit.org/sleuthkit/

Volatility

The well-known open source memory forensics framework for incident response and malware analysis.

http://www.volatilityfoundation.org/

Timeline creation

The traditional timeline analysis is generated using data extracted from the filesystem, enriched with information gathered by volatile memory analisys. The data are parsed and sorted in order to be analyzed: the end goal is to generate a snapshot of the activity done in the system including its date, the artifact involved, action and source.

Here the steps, starting from a **E01** dump and a volatile memory dump:

1. Extract filesystem bodyfile from the .E01 file (physical disk dump):

```
fls -r -m / Evidence1.E01 > Evidence1-bodyfile
```

2. Run the **timeliner** plugin against volatile memory dump using volatility, after image identification:

```
vol.py -f Evidence1-memoryraw.001 --profile=Win7SP1x86 timeliner --
output=body > Evidence1-timeliner.body
```

3. Run the **mftparser** volatility plugin, in order to spot some strange MFT activities.
    This step can generate duplicates entries against the fls output, but i think that this data can contain precious artifatcs.

```
vol.py -f Evidence1-memoryraw.001 --profile=Win7SP1x86 mftparser --
output=body > Evidence1-mftparser.body
```

4. Combine the **timeliner** and **mftparser** output files with the filesystem bodyfile

```
cat Evidence1-timeliner.body >> Evidence1-bodyfile
cat Evidence1-mftparser.body >> Evidence1-bodyfile
```

5. Extract the combined filesystem and memory timeline

```
mactime -d -b Evidence1-bodyfile 2012-04-02..2012-04-07 > Evidence1-
mactime-timeline.csv
```

6. Optionally, filter data using grep and applying the whitelist

```
grep -v -i -f Evidence1-mactime-timeline.csv > Evidence1-mactime-timeline-
final.csv
```

Supertimeline creation

The super timeline goes beyond the traditional file system timeline creation based on metadata extracted from acquired images by extending it with more sources, including more artifacts that provide valuable information to the investigation.

The technique was published in June 2010, on the SANS reading room (https://www.sans.org/reading-room/), in a paper from **Kristinn Gudjonsson** (https://www.sans.org/reading-room/whitepapers/logging/mastering-super-timeline-log2timeline-33438) as part of his **GCFA gold certification**.

Required tools

log2timeline
A tool designed to extract timestamps from various files found on a typical computer system(s) and aggregate them.

https://github.com/log2timeline/plaso

Timeline creation

Three simple steps starting from a **E01** dump:

1. Gather timeline data

```
log2timeline.py plaso.dump Evidence1.E01
```

2. Filter the timeline using **psort.py**

```
psort.py -z "UCT" -o L2tcsv plaso.dump "date > '2012-04-03 00:00:00' AND date < '2012-04-07 00:00:00'" -w plaso.csv
```

3. Optionally filter data using grep and applying the whitelist

```
grep -v -i -f whitelist.txt plaso.csv > supertimeline.csv
```

Timeline sort & colorize

Rob Lee, on SANS Digital Forensics and Incident Response Blog, has released a useful Timeline Template that can be used to automatically colorize the timeline.

The template (compatible with MS EXCEL 2007 or higher) can be downloaded here: https://blogs.sans.org/computer-forensics/files/2012/01/TIMELINE_COLOR_TEMPLATE.zip:

1. Open Timeline Color Template
2. Switch to Color Timeline worksheet/tab
3. Click on Cell A-1
4. Select 'DATA' Ribbon
5. Import Data "FROM TEXT"
6. Select the log2timeline.csv file generated in the previous step.
7. TEXT IMPORT WIZARD Will Start
   i) Step 1 -> Select Delimited ->Select NEXT
   ii) Step 2 -> Unselect Tab under Delimiters -> Select Comma under Delimiters -> Select NEXT >
   iii) Step 3 ->Select Finish
   iv) Where do you want to put the data? Simply Select OK.
8. Once imported View -> Freeze Panes -> Freeze Top Row
9. Optional Hide Columns Timezone, User, Host, Short or Desc (keep one of these), Version
10. Select HOME Ribbon
11. Select all Cells "CTRL-A"
12. In Home Ribbon -> Sort and Filter - Filter

date	time	MACB	sourcetype	type	short
39459	0.06115	MACB	Email PST	Email Read	Message 114; Attachment m57biz.xls Opened
7/20/2008	1:27:40	MACB	XP Prefetch	Last run	EXCEL.EXE-1C7SF8D6.pf: EXCEL.EXE was executed
7/20/2008	1:27:40	.AC.	NTFS $MFT	$SI [.AC.] time	C:/Program Files/Microsoft Office/Office/EXCEL.EXE
7/20/2008	1:27:30	.AC.	UserAssist key	Time of Launch	UEME_RUNPATH:C:/PROGRA~1/MICROS~2/Office/EXCEL.EXE
7/20/2008	1:28:03	..CB		Created	C:/Documents and Settings/Jean/Desktop/m57biz.xls
7/20/2008	1:28:043	MACB	NTFS $MFT	$SI [MACB] time	C:/Documents and Settings/Jean/Application Data/Microsoft/Office/Recent/Desktop.LNK
7/20/2008	1:28:03	MACB	FileExts key	Extension Change	File extension .xls opened by EXCEL.EXE
7/20/2008	1:28:03	MACB	NTFS $MFT	$SI [MACB] time	C:/windows/system32/winsvchost.exe
7/20/2008	1:28:03		SOFTWARE key	Last Written	SOFTWARE/Microsoft/Windows/CurrentVersion/Run
7/20/2008	1:27:40		Memory Process	Process Started	winsvchost.exe|1556|1032|0x02476768
7/20/2008	1:27:40		Memory Socket	Socket Opened	4|134.182.111.82:443|Protocol: 6 (TCP)|0x8162de98|||
7/20/2008	1:27:40		XP Prefetch	Last run	WINSVCHOST.EXE-1C7SF8D6.pf: EXCEL.EXE was executed
7/20/2008	1:28:03	..B.	Shortcut LNK	Created	C:/Documents and Settings/Jean/Desktop/m57biz.xls
7/20/2008	1:28:04	.A..	Shortcut LNK	Access	C:/Documents and Settings/Jean/Desktop/m57biz.xls
7/20/2008	1:28:04	MAC.	NTFS $MFT	$SI [MAC.] time	C:/Documents and Settings/Jean/Application Data/Microsoft/Office/Recent/m57biz.LNK
7/20/2008	1:28:04	.C.	NTFS $MFT	$SI [..C.] time	C:/Documents and Settings/Jean/Local Settings/History/History.IE5/MSHist012008072020080
7/20/2008	1:28:04	.C.	NTFS $MFT	$SI [..C.] time	C:/Documents and Settings/Jean/Local Settings/History/History.IE5/MSHist012008072020080
7/20/2008	1:28:04	MACB	RecentDocs key	File opened	Recently opened file of extension: .xls - value: m57biz.xls

Alphabetical Index

U

USB Storage · 79
UserAssist · 69

V

Versions · 13, 20, 38, 39, 100
Volatility · 49, 52, 55, 56, 129

Volume Shadow Copies · 37, 41, 42, 43
VSS · 37, 38, 41, 43

W

Wasted Sectors · 10
Windows Protect Storage · 74
Windows Search · 76
WordWheelQuery · 76

44756062R00080

Made in the USA
Middletown, DE
09 May 2019